"Julie Coleman explores the most salient biblical issues that prevent people in the pew from receiving, understanding, and supporting women's leadership in the church. The book oozes with biblical common sense . . . without the burden of bitterness and is safe for those exploring the issue for the first time."

—**Mimi Haddad**, president of CBE International

"Coleman has done a thorough and thoughtful treatment of this important topic. . . . She includes relatable personal stories and writes in an engaging way. Her sections on 'challenging' passages in the Bible are well researched and well argued. This is a valuable resource."

—**Dr. Gail Wallace**, cofounder of The Junia Project

"In her brilliant new book, Julie Coleman sleuths through biblical passages traditionally thought to limit women. Not only does she extract their original meanings, Julie pulls back the curtain on both the cultural and historical happenings of the New Testament. Her discoveries . . . will shift how you think about God's plans and purposes for women."

—**Linda Evans Shepherd**, best-selling author of *Praying God's Promises*, founder and leader of the Advanced Writers and Speakers Association, and CEO of Right to the Heart Ministries

"A fresh, liberating, and biblical wind blows through every page of this long-needed work."

—**Rev. Dawn Damon**, author of *The Freedom Challenge: 60 Days to Untie the Cords That Bind You*

"[*On Purpose*] is at once biblically faithful, academically sound, gracious toward those with whom she disagrees, and accessible to a broad readership."

—**Ronald W. Pierce**, professor of biblical and theological studies at Biola University, editor of *Discovering Biblical Equality*, and author of *Partners in Marriage and Ministry*

"This book is a breath of refreshment for all believers who've wrestled with the roles of women—especially women with the gift and calling of leadership. Savor this well-researched book and walk confidently in your God-given calling."

—**Debbie W. Wilson**, author of *Little Women, Big God*; Bible teacher; retired biblical counselor; and cofounder of Lighthouse Ministries of Raleigh

"What sets Julie's book apart from others on similar topics is heart. Julie writes with kindness and common sense and with her eyes on the gospel of Jesus."

—**Margaret Mowczko**, theologian and blogger at MargMowczko.com

"While some of Coleman's research may initially surprise you, it will also be an aha moment that will move our culture forward."

—**Monica Schmelter**, TV host for TCN's *Bridges*, author, and speaker

"I recommend this read to women who are prayerful about digging deeper into Scripture to discover the life God designed them to live."

—**Linda Goldfarb**, international speaker, board-certified Christian life coach, and author of the award-winning LINKED: Quick Guide to Personalities series

ON
PURPOSE

ON PURPOSE

*Understanding
God's Freedom for Women
Through Scripture*

Julie Zine Coleman

KREGEL
PUBLICATIONS

Published by Kregel Publications, a division of Kregel Inc., 2450 Oak Industrial Dr. NE, Grand Rapids, MI 49505. www.kregel.com.

Library of Congress Cataloging-in-Publication Data
Names: Zine Coleman, Julie, 1957- author.
Title: On purpose : understanding God's freedom for women through scripture
   / Julie Zine Coleman.
Description: Grand Rapids : Kregel Publications, [2022] | Includes
   bibliographical references.
Subjects: LCSH: Women--Biblical teaching. | Sex role--Biblical teaching. |
   Liberty--Biblical teaching.
Classification: LCC BS680.W7 Z56 2022 (print) | LCC BS680.W7 (ebook) |
   DDC 220.8/3054--dc23/eng/20211207
LC record available at https://lccn.loc.gov/2021053161
LC ebook record available at https://lccn.loc.gov/2021053162

ISBN 978-0-8254-4707-5, print
ISBN 978-0-8254-7755-3, epub
ISBN 978-0-8254-6907-7, Kindle

Printed in the United States of America
22 23 24 25 26 27 28 29 30 31 / 5 4 3 2 1

To my New Hope Chapel family, who have given me wings to fly.
I never take the freedom to exercise my spiritual gifts for granted.
You live out the kingdom of God in the love and support you so
generously give to each other.
I am grateful.

Contents

Introduction

He cornered me in the snack bar after chapel. At the camp director's request, I had just led the singing that evening for the new group of campers and counselors at Boys Camp. I had been initially reluctant to lead in front of a group of men, having been taught that the Bible restricted women in that way. But I was assured it would be fine, because, after all, the camp leadership was *asking* me to do it.

But the speaker didn't see it that way. Beet red in the face, barely controlling his anger, he confronted me. Why would I ever think it appropriate to lead men? He then went on to lecture me on what Scripture teaches about women (like I hadn't heard it my entire life) and had me reduced to tears by the time he was done.

I tried to explain why I was leading, but he was having none of it. That was it for my new assignment. The camp did without a competent song leader for the rest of the two weeks.

It was the 1970s. This was one of several incidents that made me question the many restrictions placed on women in most conservative denominations at that time. Please understand, I knew the Scriptures cited for those limitations almost as well as John 3:16. However, I was wired to be a leader, which caused me to feel as though I was constantly crashing into a glass ceiling. I often wondered why God would have made me the way he did, if I had to worry every time I used my spiritual gifts. I lived in constant fear of crossing the line between appropriate and inappropriate.

Much has changed culturally since my college days. Women now hold key leadership positions in business, in politics, and enjoy respect by society in general. Equality has been reached on many levels. But not in the church. It has been said that the church always arrives thirty years late and out of breath. But in this case, traditional roles have been dictated by Scripture, which is timeless in its principles and far above any cultural determination. Right? But does Scripture really teach limitations? Or is the traditional position in reality an *interpretation* of God's Word, subject to human error or misunderstanding?

I had to wonder about that possibility in my early years, because every group drew their lines in the sand in different places. In some churches (like mine), women wore head coverings and kept silent. They couldn't speak in a church business meeting or serve on a committee with men. In other churches, women could pray out loud or give their testimony, but not preach. Of course, if you were a missionary, all bets were off. Many women in the field spent their lives teaching men and women alike, since there was no man to lead at their location.

Then there was the seeming inconsistency of God himself. If his will was for women never to lead men, why would he choose, for example, Deborah to be judge over Israel? Why would he use Priscilla to teach the great preacher Apollos, patiently correcting his misunderstandings and leading him to truth? Why did Jesus make Mary Magdalene the first witness to his resurrection, when a woman's testimony wasn't even admissible in a Jewish court? In view of all these examples, wasn't God violating his own rules?

There were also discrepancies in the application of the "rules." In my early adult years, I noticed that sometimes women *were* allowed to "teach" men. No one seemed concerned when men sang hymns full of theology written by Fanny Crosby or read books by Elisabeth Elliot or Catherine Marshall. A friend of mine attended a conservative Bible college where Elisabeth Elliot was invited to speak for a chapel. In order to make this acceptable, the authorities removed the podium and replaced it with a music stand.

It all seemed so arbitrary.

My own understanding of God's Word on the matter has morphed slowly over the years. I married a wonderful man who loves and knows his Bible better than anyone I know. Over the years, Steve inspired me to study those limiting passages in earnest. What did they really mean? To my surprise, when I did, what I found in my research was very different from what I had always been taught.

Steve has always interpreted those passages differently than our denomination did, and from the beginning saw no need to limit his wife in any way. Contrary to what *I* believed about marriage on our wedding day, we have always functioned as a team, a true partnership rather than a hierarchy. As the Lord opened up ministry opportunities for me over the years, Steve has been my biggest cheerleader. Never once was he threatened by my strong personality. Never once did he remind me to "keep my place," as I had previously been told. He has remained consistent in selflessly looking out for my best interests.

Interpretation is limited by an interpreter's perspective. Anyone studying Scripture has factors that can keep them from a correct understanding. There are the basic beliefs that we have been taught from an early age, be they right or wrong. Those things become the foundation and filter for any additional knowledge we may gain. Our tightly held assumptions are the lens through which we see the world. Our experiences chime in as well. Past hurts or successes will influence how we receive information. In part, those things have made us into who we are today.

So, while Scripture is God's Word, divinely inspired, accurate and powerful, human interpretation is not. Interpreters are always affected by their core beliefs.

We used to joke in seminary: "I love it when Scripture backs me up." But seriously, *we were joking.* When we approach Scripture with something to prove, we tend to see things that aren't even there. We can take verses out of context in order to justify what we already believe. The chance of bad interpretation is exponentially larger when we've already decided what we think before studying the text.

So how do we avoid that pitfall? Keep ourselves from putting words into God's mouth? Refrain from interjecting what we think into what the Bible says?

It's not easy. I ran into that problem when writing my first book, *Unexpected Love.* Many of the stories I covered were already so familiar to me. This was especially true of Martha and Mary. I'd always heard: Martha was bad. She should not have been working in the kitchen with Jesus teaching in the living room. Mary was good. She sat at Jesus's feet and hung on His every word. But something had always bothered me about that interpretation. Hospitality was commanded in Mosaic law. Martha was merely obeying Scripture. So why then would Jesus criticize Martha for whipping up a dinner?

Before I began studying the Martha passage, I spent time in prayer, asking God to help me put aside what I'd always heard. As I dug in, I carefully noted each detail Luke provided. I researched the original Greek text. I noticed repeated phrases and important words. I spent a lot of time looking at the context of the story, and how it fit into the whole. My quest was to see, really see, what was *there* in black-and-white.

Commentaries were a help in finding other things to research that could assist me in my understanding. So were books explaining first-century Jewish history, customs, and culture. I tried not to rely heavily on extrabiblical sources, though, since much of their content is also affected by human interpretation. As learned as those authors might be, they can still contradict each other. My primary dependence was on the Holy Spirit to teach and guide me as I searched for the meaning of the story.

In the end, the Lord did give me new insight into that puzzling interaction between Jesus and Martha. It came through systematic study of the text, searching for the principal point the author intended to make. For the most part, that careful process helped me put the noise of my biases and previous beliefs aside, so I could hear the Holy Spirit guide me to something fresh.

My passion for the subject of this book comes from a concern that we have gotten it wrong. I ache for future generations whose culture has moved on, giving them a freedom in secular society that the church will not allow. I have seen women told to stay in abusive marriages while their church leadership tiptoes around the abusers, refusing to hold them accountable. I have seen too many people leave Christian fellowship because of their disillusionment with how women are treated by the body. Worst of all—I have seen women walk away from God, because they believe he thinks of them as second-class citizens in his kingdom.

In this book, I want to take you on a journey through the passages that are traditionally thought to limit women. We are going to look, really look, at what is written there for us. We will (as much as is humanly possible) put aside what we have previously heard or thought and start each passage with a clean slate.

It doesn't matter what I think. What matters is what the Word of God says. You have a personal responsibility to figure this out with the help of the Holy Spirit. This issue isn't only about half the church. How we interpret these passages affects everyone. Because if we are limiting women unnecessarily, we are handicapping God's church, keeping it from functioning in the way he designed it. We would be endeavoring to walk on only one leg, when we were given two.

Before we get started, I need to add one last thing. I will be sharing some of my past experiences as well as others' that negatively portray brothers or sisters in Christ. Those stories are to present the issues and draw the reader in to what we are about to study. They stand as examples in how applying a bad interpretation can produce terrible results.

In no way do I mean to judge or disrespect those depicted. I believe with all my heart that their strong convictions and resulting actions came from their understanding of certain texts. They were trying to remain true to what they believed Scripture teaches. I get it.

I am not angry for those incidents from my past. I am thankful for an upbringing that emphasized the importance of the Bible and taking personal responsibility to study it for myself. I was well-loved in my church and camp. A love for God and desire to obey him was modeled for me frequently. I love the people of God. As messy as that can get at times.

Now more than ever, we need to get to the bottom of these passages, because the debate rages on. The only way we can have peace about what to think is to study these passages for ourselves. I hope this book inspires you to look for the timeless principles in Scripture that are true for any culture, because the truth always sets us free. What does God have to say about women and marriage, their inherent value, and how they are to use their gifts? Get ready to dig in. You might well be surprised.

Chapter 1

Was Woman Created with an Inherently Different Nature Than Man's?

Then God said, "Let Us make mankind in Our image, according to Our likeness; and let them rule over the fish of the sea and over the birds of the sky and over the livestock and over all the earth, and over every crawling thing that crawls on the earth." So God created man in His own image, in the image of God He created him; male and female He created them. God blessed them; and God said to them, "Be fruitful and multiply, and fill the earth, and subdue it; and rule over the fish of the sea and over the birds of the sky and over every living thing that moves on the earth." Then God said, "Behold, I have given you every plant yielding seed that is on the surface of all the earth, and every tree which has fruit yielding seed; it shall be food for you; and to every animal of the earth and to every bird of the sky and to everything that moves on the earth which has life, I have given every green plant for food"; and it was so. And God saw all that He had made, and behold, it was very good. And there was evening and there was morning, the sixth day.

And so the heavens and the earth were completed, and all their heavenly lights. By the seventh day God completed His work which He had done, and He rested on the seventh day from all His work which He had done. Then God blessed the seventh day and sanctified it, because on it He rested from all His work which God had created and made.

This is the account of the heavens and the earth when they were created, in the day that the LORD God made earth and heaven. Now no shrub of the field was yet on the earth, and no plant of the field had yet sprouted, for the LORD God had not sent rain upon the earth, and there was no man to cultivate the ground. But a mist used to rise from the earth and water the whole surface of the ground. Then the LORD God formed the man of dust from the ground, and breathed into his nostrils the breath of life; and the man became a living person. The LORD God planted a garden toward the east, in Eden; and there He placed the man whom He had formed. Out of the ground the LORD God caused every tree to grow that is pleasing to the sight and good for food; the tree of life was also in the midst of the garden, and the tree of the knowledge of good and evil.

Now a river flowed out of Eden to water the garden; and from there it divided and became four rivers. The name of the first is Pishon; it flows around the whole land of Havilah, where there is gold. The gold of that land is good; the bdellium and the onyx stone are there as well. The name of the second river is Gihon; it flows around the whole land of Cush. The name of the third river is Tigris; it flows east of Assyria. And the fourth river is the Euphrates.

Then the LORD God took the man and put him in the Garden of Eden to cultivate it and tend it. The LORD God commanded the man, saying, "From any tree of the garden you may freely eat; but from the tree of the knowledge of good and evil you shall not eat, for on the day that you eat from it you will certainly die."

Then the LORD God said, "It is not good for the man to be alone; I will make him a helper suitable for him." And out of the ground the LORD God formed every animal of the field and every bird of the sky, and brought them to the man to see what he would call them; and whatever the man called a living creature, that was its name. The man gave names to all the livestock, and to the birds of the sky, and to every animal of the field, but for Adam there was not found a helper suitable for him. So the LORD God caused a deep sleep to fall upon the man, and he slept; then He took one of his ribs and closed up the flesh at that place. And the LORD God fashioned into a woman the rib which He had taken from the man, and brought her to the man. Then the man said,

> "At last this is bone of my bones,
> And flesh of my flesh;
> She shall be called 'woman,'
> Because she was taken out of man."

For this reason a man shall leave his father and his mother, and be joined to his wife; and they shall become one flesh. And the man and his wife were both naked, but they were not ashamed.

—Genesis 1:26–2:25

Focus on Genesis 1–2

I was preparing for a coming women's retreat with an area church when I received a troubling call from their pastor. Mind you, I was not a new speaker for them and had previously received nothing but positive feedback. But the pastor was troubled about my newly published book, *Unexpected Love: God's Heart Revealed through Jesus' Conversations with Women*. The coming retreat would be drawn from the content of that book as per their request. But now he worried that my material would contradict certain positions in their doctrinal statement.

Wait . . . what?

I inquired: had he read the book? He hadn't. But he had read the four-page introduction. I racked my brain trying to think of what was in there that could possibly be upsetting. I finally asked.

He told me, "You wrote that Jesus came to set women free."

I was puzzled. "You don't think that Jesus came to set women free?" I asked.

"Well, it depends on what you mean by free," he explained. He then reminded me that God had created women to be under men's authority from the very beginning in Genesis 1–2. So, in that sense, he reasoned, women would never be "free." Man's headship was God's designed, natural order.

It was one of those conversations I would replay over and over in my head for some time. *Does* the creation account indicate that God designed women to be subservient? Was there a hierarchy in the relationship between men and women from the beginning? Were women created with an inherently different nature than men?

Genesis is a great place to start looking for God's true intent for women, because it is only there we get a brief glimpse of what the world was like without sin. We see the first humans near the very end of the creation account. All of earth's flora and fauna have been brought into being. Now comes the crowning moment, when God creates a being far different than anything else. "So God created man in His own image, in the image of God He created him; male and female He created them" (Gen. 1:27).

What Does It Mean to Be Created in the Image of God?

Images can be pretty realistic. When I was a little girl, my friend Chrissie and I went to the town carnival with her dad. For the first time, we were allowed to go through the fun house all by ourselves. We felt very grown-up as we handed our tickets to the ticket taker, and hurried past the enormous man in a gorilla costume stationed at the door. As we began to navigate the maze in the first room, Chrissie suddenly grabbed my arm in fear. "That gorilla is following us," she whispered. We took off running.

No matter how quickly we rushed through each new room, we could not widen the gap between us and the gorilla. It was terrifying. The worst panic came as we entered the room of mirrors. We could see the exit doorway's reflection, but every time we tried to go through it, we only banged into glass. The image was so real it kept us fooled for excruciatingly long moments. Finally, by feeling our way along the mirrored walls, we found the real exit and made our escape.

The gorilla gave up the chase as we rushed outside, back to the safety of Chrissie's dad. I was never so happy to see an adult in my life.

As we discovered with those mirrors, an image can be convincing, but it is merely a likeness of the real thing. Both man and woman were created in the image of God. Both would reflect the reality of God to the rest of his creation.

The original audience of the Genesis account would not have had trouble understanding this "image" terminology at all. They were familiar with the ancient practice of conquering rulers leaving statues of themselves in acquired far-reaching lands. Those images stood as constant reminders of who was in charge, a representative of that ruler's power in their absence.[1]

While the rest of God's creation evidenced his existence and power, humans alone were created in his *image*. They would reflect the Creator to the rest of creation, functioning as a representative of the real thing. Their very existence would, in ways other than the creation around them, show the nature of God.

Then the Lord told the man and woman *how* they were to represent him: "Be fruitful and multiply, and fill the earth, and subdue it; and rule over the fish of the sea and over the birds of the sky and over every living thing that moves on the earth" (Gen. 1:28). God's representatives were to have dominion over the rest of creation. Both of them.

They simultaneously received this charge from the Lord. They were to rule together. And God saw that it was very good. Then on the seventh day, he rested.

Does the Fact That Woman Was Created to Be Man's "Helper" Mean She Was Subordinate to Him?

In Genesis 2, the narrator provides a closer look into the same events of chapter 1, furnishing greater detail about humankind. God builds man from the dust of the ground and breathes life into him. He fashions a perfect place for man to live, a garden with water, trees, and plants to provide for his physical needs. He sets man in the garden to cultivate it. All is his to enjoy.

But there is one caveat: in the midst of plenty, God places the tree of the knowledge of good and evil. From that tree, man was never to eat. With his instruction, God adds a stern warning: "On the day that you eat from it you will certainly die" (Gen. 2:17).[2]

---

1. Richard Hess, "Equality With and Without Innocence," *Discovering Biblical Equality: Complementarity Without Hierarchy*, ed. Ronald W. Pierce, Rebecca Merrill Groothuis, and Gordon D. Fee (Downers Grove, IL: IVP Academic, 2005), 81.
2. Was the tree placed in the garden as some kind of temptation? James 1:13 tells us, "No one is to say when he is tempted, 'I am being tempted by God'; for God

But God is not quite finished. In order for man to multiply and fill the earth, there must be a counterpart. Had the man understood what was missing? It's interesting that before creating the woman, God first gave man the huge task of naming every living creature.[3] Because as he does, a realization seems to dawn on him: while each animal, from the birds of the sky to the beasts of the field, has its suitable mate, he does not.

The man has discovered himself to be unique in God's creation. He needs a *helper*.

In the English language, a *helper* is an assistant. It is someone to come along and do another's bidding, managing the smaller tasks that will enable the more important person to complete a job.

My children loved to assist me in making Christmas cookies when they were little. They wanted to help in every stage of baking: mixing the dough, rolling it out, cutting out shapes, and after the baking was done, decorating their creations.

When they were finished "helping" me, flour covered the entire kitchen table and much of the floor. The cookies were inconsistent: the super thin ones burned, and those too thick did not bake all the way through. And the royal icing? A nightmare. I would find traces of hardened icing for days. The capacity four young children had to make a mess while helping was unbelievable. And in the end, as proud as they were of their finished products, the cookies were substandard at best. Sometimes "help" is not all it's cracked up to be.

Is that what the original word *helper* (Hebrew: *ezer*) meant? Was the woman created to be a mere assistant for the more important man? Was their relationship designed to be the lesser serving the greater?

---

cannot be tempted by evil, and He Himself does not tempt anyone." So then why was it there? It seems likely that it stood as a reminder to man that while he reflected God's image, he was not God. It was a continual reminder that he served a power far greater than himself. He was a part of God's creation, not a deity. The tree provided a physical, visual contrast between God and man.

3. Did he do this to create in Adam an interest in a partner? It was during the naming of the animals that the man realized he was alone. He saw his need. It was only then that God created woman.

When we aren't sure of the full meaning of a word in the original ancient language, it's good practice to investigate other places that word is used in Scripture. There are plenty of other examples of helper (*ezer*) available to us.

God is often described as an *ezer*:

- "There is no one like the God of Jeshurun, who rides the heavens to your *help*, and the clouds in His majesty" (Deut. 33:26, emphasis mine).
- God promised his people: "'Do not fear, for I am with you; do not be afraid, for I am your God. I will strengthen you, I will also *help* you, I will uphold you with My righteous right hand.' . . . Those who contend with you will be as nothing and will perish" (Isa. 41:10–11, emphasis mine).

There are many more instances of God's help in the Old Testament. Each time, he is coming to the rescue of those who are weak and in need.

Great armies are called *ezers* as well:

- In Isaiah, God rebukes Israel for trusting in a neighboring army for assistance instead of him: "Woe to those who go down to Egypt for *help* and rely on horses, and trust in chariots because there are many and in horsemen because they are very strong, but they do not look to the Holy One of Israel, nor seek the Lord!" (Isa. 31:1, emphasis mine).
- During the reign of King Amaziah, the nation was in dire straits. There was no help to be found: "For the Lord saw the misery of Israel, which was very bitter; for there was neither bond nor free spared, nor was there any *helper* for Israel" (2 Kings 14:26, emphasis mine).

There are other instances of Israel seeking the *help* of a strong nation, enlisting military aid against an enemy they could not defeat on their own (see 1 Kings 20:16; Isa. 30:5).

There is no indication in the Old Testament that an *ezer* involves subservience. Would God be considered subservient to those he has come to save? No more than an army capable of coming alongside Israel to rescue them from their enemies would be thought of as weak.

So while the English word *helper* can have connotations of an underling or weaker assistant, the original Hebrew word *ezer* does not.[4]

There is no indication from which we should infer the woman was originally designed to be subordinate to man's authority as a subservient assistant, at least from what is in the text thus far. She would stand by his side to co-rule the earth with him, just as they were charged to do in Genesis 1:28.

Did the Fact That the Man Gave a Name to the Woman Mean He Was to Rule over Her?

After meeting her for the first time, the man identifies his female counterpart as "woman."[5] He later begins to call her "Eve" in Genesis 3:20, "because she was the mother of all the living." Could the fact that he felt free to give her a name show his dominion over her? After all, he had just finished naming the animals, over which he was given dominion.

In other places in the Bible, naming someone does not necessarily indicate authority over them. For example, later in Genesis, Abraham's concubine, Hagar, has an encounter with God after fleeing

---

4. It has been suggested that the Hebrew word directly following *ezer*, *kenegdo*, could be translated as "under." The root word, *neged*, is used 150 times in the Old Testament. The only context in which it is translated as "under" in the NASB is 2 Sam. 12:12, where God promises judgment: "Indeed you did it secretly, but I will do this thing before all Israel, and under the sun" (NASB1995). Obviously, God is not placing himself under the authority of the sun. The phrase is meant to communicate that God's judgment will be given in broad daylight. *Kenegdo* in every other instance is translated as "over against" or "in front of" or "in the presence of." There is no indication that *ezer kenegdo* would indicate Eve or the help she would provide as under Adam's authority. The best literal translation is "helper corresponding to."

5. The Hebrew word *adam* has not yet been used as a proper name (and is not until Gen. 4:25; until then, *adam* indicates general humankind). The noun *adam* is the masculine form of the word *adamah*, which literally means *ground* or *earth*.

her mistress Sarah's mistreatment. The Lord tells Hagar that she will give birth to a son and gives her a reassuring glimpse of his future long life. In response, Hagar "called the name of the LORD who spoke to her, 'You are a God who sees'" (Gen. 16:13 NASB1995). *El Roi.*

Did giving him a name indicate Hagar had dominion over God? Of course not.

The man sure didn't seem to think the woman was a companion to be dominated: "At last this is bone of my bones, and flesh of my flesh" (Gen. 2:23). This statement doesn't indicate a sense of weakness or belief that she was in any way less than him. There is nothing to note beyond an expression of mutual equality. If we want to know why he named her *woman*, we only have to look at the text: "She shall be called 'woman,' because she was taken out of man" (Gen. 2:23). The name itself, while noting a diversity in sex, actually reflects the unity in their essence.

God's final creation was someone just like him, made in the image of God, meant to share the responsibility in subduing the earth. The narrator confirms this by interjecting: "For this reason a man shall leave his father and his mother, and be joined to his wife; and they shall become one flesh" (Gen. 2:24). The division God created when he took a part out of man would be restored when the two become one again.

One. It would be a harmonious relationship from the start.

Does the Order in Which Man and Woman Were Created Indicate Anything About God's Intentions for Their Relationship?

There's one more issue that we need to address. Did the fact that man was created first indicate he was the most important or meant to be the dominant one? After all, in the Old Testament, the position of firstborn son was highly prized. He received the largest portion of the inheritance and became the ruling patriarch of the family when the father died. So wasn't the man then more privileged or valuable in God's eyes as his "firstborn"?

A look at the rest of Genesis (remember, context!) does not support this idea. While firstborn sons often had a place of preference in Jewish family lineages, this is not always consistent in the biblical narrative. God certainly did not bless or elevate the firstborns over their brothers in any of the patriarchs' families. The family line (which would eventually produce Jesus Christ) went through Seth in the next generation, who was the third child of Adam and Eve. Later on, Abraham's second son Isaac and his descendants received the everlasting covenant with God, promised someday to become his chosen nation. Isaac's son Jacob was chosen over his older brother Esau. God placed Jacob's son Joseph in a position to rule over his brothers, and he was the eleventh out of twelve. It would be hard to prove from the rest of Genesis that God gave preference or greater value to a firstborn (or first-created) human.

Also, man and woman were not the only ones created on the sixth day. The cattle, creeping things, and beasts of the earth were created first. So, assuming creation order was an indication of superiority would make the animals the most important. Which obviously was not the case, since they were not created in the image of God. Humanity was the crowning glory over *all creation*.

As we leave this sixth day of creation, we can look back to see a perfect setting, inhabited by perfect people who perfectly reflected the image of God. There is nothing in their relationship or circumstances to keep them from living as one in perfect harmony.

But the tranquility wouldn't last for long. With the advent of sin, all of that perfection quickly dissolved. Life as they first knew it would be forever altered. In the next chapter, we will look at what changed after the fall. The introduction of sin was most definitely a game changer.

Good News for Today

While people have used the creation account in Genesis 1–2 as proof that woman was different from man in how she reflected God's image or in her position in their relationship, evidence of that is simply *not in the text.* Teachers who promote that idea rarely quote Genesis 1:27–28. They stick to chapter 2. It is a case of taking the one chapter out of the context of the whole book. Never a good idea.

If we see chapter 2 in light of what was told to us in chapter 1, we know there was no hierarchy. Both were created in the image of God. Both man and woman were given the same responsibilities. The woman was described by the man as "bone of my bones, flesh of my flesh." Both were formed from the dust of the ground. And God taking a part from Adam's side guaranteed she was just like him, outside of their sex differences.

Even without the context of Genesis 1:27–28, it would take a good deal of conjecture (or predetermined assumptions) to read hierarchy into chapter 2. But chapter 2 does not stand alone. It is part of a whole—the whole creation account and the whole book of Genesis.

Man and woman are identified in Genesis 2:21–24 as being of the same essence. Cut from the same cloth, so to speak. As Gilbert Bilezikian observes:

> God had recourse to a strange cloning operation that demonstrated beyond the shadow of a doubt the essential identity between man and woman. Had Eve been made out of the ground, there might have existed ambiguity about the integrity of her human nature. After all, animals had also been taken from the ground. . . . However, since she was taken from Adam, no confusion about her full participation in his humanity was possible. She was made from the same material as his own body. From one being, God made two persons.[6]

After interpreting the meaning of a passage, it is important to determine the principle that it teaches. Preachers call this the *Big Idea.* It is a timeless truth extracted from a passage that is not connected to any particular culture or time period: a principle that can

---

6. Gilbert Bilezikian, *Beyond Sex Roles: What the Bible Says about a Woman's Place in the Church and Family,* 3rd ed. (Grand Rapids: Baker Academic, 2006), 23.

be applied to someone who lives in a developing country as well as those in a metropolitan city.

What is the principle that summarizes Genesis 1 and 2? Man and woman were made from the same essence, in the image of God, charged to multiply and subdue the earth. The only limitation mentioned was the command not to eat from the tree of the knowledge of good and evil.

But within that framework of essence and image, there are endless possibilities of divergence. The uniqueness within all of humanity is a wonderful expression of God's boundless creativity. This should prompt us to rethink any culturally driven stereotypes about males and females. We can't discount God's varied expression and squeeze his creation into a box we were never meant to construct.

Many of our preconceived ideas of what makes a man a man and a woman a woman come from culture, rather than the Word of God. I have friends who abandoned some of those cultural expectations; they structured their marriage and family based on their God-given gifts. She is a math prodigy and has a great job in government security. He is a nurturer and stays home with their small children to give them full-time care.

For sure it raises some eyebrows. But they are partners, a team, working together to fill family needs through the strengths God gave them.

My husband used to get a little irritated when I would go out of town for a few days and people at church would joke, "I guess you are getting to know Mrs. Swanson this weekend!" He is proficient in the kitchen and has no problem preparing a good meal. It was a bit insulting to assume he was domestically helpless because he was a man.

People need to be allowed to be who they were created to be. As the old proverb states, "As a twig is bent, so grows the tree."[7] To insist on stereotypical roles is akin to forcing a left-handed child to write with her right hand (as past generations have done).

---

7. Alexander Pope, the eighteenth-century poet, is credited with coining the phrase.

Males and females share the same nature. Created in the image of God. Capable of exercising dominion over the earth. To limit women or men to culturally expected roles is to fail to recognize what God may have created them to be. In my experience, the church tends to hold on to culture that has moved on and fails to separate our spiritual understanding from a culturally inspired mentality. Rather than being at the forefront of positive change, we end up following those ever-changing norms with our feet dragging.

We can't allow societal expectations to dictate what we think about men and women. We must define the nature of man and woman from what the biblical text tells us. We need to embrace the strengths and weaknesses that make up each individual.

We must always work to pull principles out of Scripture that can work in any society. Because when we mistakenly attach the Bible to a bygone culture, God's Word becomes extraneous to contemporary lives. God is relevant to any time period and any culture. He is bigger than societal norms or time-driven ideals.

In the following chapters, you will find that what some would define as biblical manhood or womanhood does not stand up to how God interacted with people in Scripture, both male and female. He dealt with each person uniquely. He gave them different strengths and weaknesses. He met them where they were and moved them forward according to his plan.

God is not limited by our cultural preferences. Nor are men and women (created as unique individuals, of the same essence). Anything other than that principle is not from the text of Genesis 1 and 2.

Chapter 2

Did God Establish a Hierarchy for Marriages After the Fall?

Now the serpent was more cunning than any animal of the field which the LORD God had made. And he said to the woman, "Has God really said, 'You shall not eat from any tree of the garden'?" The woman said to the serpent, "From the fruit of the trees of the garden we may eat; but from the fruit of the tree which is in the middle of the garden, God has said, 'You shall not eat from it or touch it, or you will die.'" The serpent said to the woman, "You certainly will not die! For God knows that on the day you eat from it your eyes will be opened, and you will become like God, knowing good and evil." When the woman saw that the tree was good for food, and that it was a delight to the eyes, and that the tree was desirable to make one wise, she took some of its fruit and ate; and she also gave some to her husband with her, and he ate. Then the eyes of both of them were opened, and they knew that they were naked; and they sewed fig leaves together and made themselves waist coverings.

Now they heard the sound of the LORD God walking in the garden in the cool of the day, and the man and his wife hid themselves from the presence of the LORD God among the trees of the garden. Then the LORD God called to the man, and said to him, "Where are you?" He said, "I heard the sound of You in the garden, and I was afraid because I was naked; so I hid myself." And He said, "Who told you that you were naked? Have you eaten from the tree from which I commanded you not to eat?" The man said, "The woman whom You gave to be with me, she gave me some of the fruit of the tree, and I ate." Then the LORD God said to the woman, "What is this that you have done?" And the woman said, "The serpent deceived me, and I ate." Then the LORD God said to the serpent,

> "Because you have done this,
> Cursed are you more than all the livestock,
> And more than any animal of the field;
> On your belly you shall go,
> And dust you shall eat
> All the days of your life;
> And I will make enemies
> Of you and the woman,
> And of your offspring and her Descendant;
> He shall bruise you on the head,
> And you shall bruise Him on the heel."

To the woman He said,

> "I will greatly multiply
> Your pain in childbirth,
> In pain you shall deliver children;
> Yet your desire will be for your husband,
> And he shall rule over you."

Then to Adam He said, "Because you have listened to the voice of your wife, and have eaten from the tree about which I commanded you, saying, 'You shall not eat from it';

> Cursed is the ground because of you;
> With hard labor you shall eat from it
> All the days of your life.
> Both thorns and thistles it shall grow for you;
> Yet you shall eat the plants of the field;
> By the sweat of your face
> You shall eat bread,
> Until you return to the ground,
> Because from it you were taken;

> For you are dust,
> And to dust you shall return."

Now the man named his wife Eve, because she was the mother of all the living. And the Lord God made garments of skin for Adam and his wife, and clothed them.

Then the Lord God said, "Behold, the man has become like one of Us, knowing good and evil; and now, he might reach out with his hand, and take fruit also from the tree of life, and eat, and live forever"—therefore the Lord God sent him out of the Garden of Eden, to cultivate the ground from which he was taken. So He drove the man out; and at the east of the Garden of Eden He stationed the cherubim and the flaming sword which turned every direction to guard the way to the tree of life.

—Genesis 3

Focus on Genesis 3

The soon-to-be-married young woman sat on my back porch, frustration written on her face. The previous evening, she and her fiancé had been in premarital counseling with a couple from her church. The subject for the evening had been submission: specifically, how a wife should submit to her husband. The older couple had supplied examples from their marriage, and my friend found them troubling.

"I always let my husband pick the restaurant when we go out after church," they were told. "And when he told me I needed to clean the lint trap before drying every load, I did it . . . even though I don't think it needs it *every* time."

My friend was bothered by their version of submission and its long-term implications. "Is the husband always supposed to have the last word?" she asked me. "Is this the consequence of the fall, that even though I have an opinion, he should determine every outcome?"

What transpired in Genesis 3, specifically God telling Eve that her husband would rule over her, has frequently been interpreted as God's curse on Eve: a punishment for eating the fruit of the forbidden tree. Because she sinned, and in the process, took her husband down with her, she would now forever be under his authority.

But is that really what happened? A careful look at Genesis 3 yields a very different story.

What Exactly Happened in the Fall?

The trouble began with a surprise encounter. For the very first time, completely innocent woman and man have their first brush with pure evil. The serpent (Satan) shows himself for the first time with the intention of destroying the perfection of God's created images.[1]

---

1. Rev. 20:2 calls him "the serpent of old, who is the devil and Satan."

The ensuing conversation between the serpent and Eve is filled with deceptive misquotes and misinformation. The serpent begins with a question for Eve: "Has God really said, 'You shall not eat from any tree of the garden'?" (Gen. 3:1). The inquiry sounds so innocent. Guileless Eve attempts to set the record straight.

"From the fruit of the trees of the garden we may eat; but from the fruit of the tree which is in the middle of the garden, God has said, 'You shall not eat from it or touch it, or you will die,'" she tells him (vv. 2–3).

Interestingly, Eve has made two changes to God's original command. First, she fails to specifically name the Tree of the Knowledge of Good and Evil. There is no indication she knows what that tree represents. Second, she adds to the prohibition: "you shall not eat from it *or touch it*." Was Eve just making stuff up? Or did she truly think that was what God had said?

Scripture doesn't tell us how Eve initially got her information. We know she was not present when God gave Adam the instruction (see Gen. 2:16–17). There is no record of God speaking to Eve about this. Genesis does not make a point of where Eve heard the command: from God or from Adam.

So, one would presume that Adam had communicated God's command to her. Did he fail to adequately name the tree? Did he add the extra warning to not even touch the tree to keep her from stepping over the line to disobedience and death?

It is also interesting how Eve states the consequences: *You will die.* Both God and the serpent use the phrase *certainly die.* The words translated *certainly die* are actually a colloquial phrase in the original Hebrew, called a Hebraism. If translated word for word, it would read "dying you shall die." The two verbs together (in two different tenses) serve to intensify the verb. This grammatical construction is not uncommon in the Old Testament. However, while God used that Hebraism in his original command, Eve does not.

But Satan does.

His next remark was similarly telling. "For God knows on the day you eat from it your eyes will be opened, and you will be like God, *knowing good and evil*" (3:5, emphasis mine). Note that Eve never mentioned the name of the tree, or even voiced the words "good and evil."

Satan seems to know more about God's command than Eve.

How? It seems likely that at the time God was talking to Adam, Satan was close by, listening for something he could use to destroy God's new creation—to corrupt what was perfectly made in his image. He certainly had his strategy prepared as he approached Eve. Did he choose to tempt her (rather than Adam) because she had received the mandate only secondhand?

We don't know. But we do know that Eve took the bait. She bit into the forbidden fruit, then handed it to Adam, who was standing next to her. He ate from the fruit as well.

How Did God Respond to Their Sin?

In that moment, everything changed. The first indication of a radical shift is their sudden awareness of their nakedness and quick attempt to cover their shame (see Gen. 3:7).[2] Satan's promise proved to be nothing but fraudulent. Rather than becoming like God, they had marred the image of him they had been created to reflect. Their sudden knowledge was not a bonus, because the evil they now knew was not from God. So much for being like him—their only change had been becoming less than they were.

Suddenly awkward and ill at ease with each other, they sew leaves together to cover themselves. Their former security and oneness is now consumed by mistrust and alienation. Not only has their relationship with each other changed, but they are also now ill at ease with God. Rather than welcoming his presence, they hide among the trees as he approaches. For the very first time in the Genesis account, they are afraid.[3]

---

2. The word used here for naked is actually a wordplay in the Hebrew: The serpent was more crafty (*arum*, shrewd) and Adam and Eve were naked (*arummim*). Their former nakedness illustrated their lack of knowledge: they were less crafty.
3. Walter Brueggemann notes that "I was afraid" in verse 10 is later the same response of other Old Testament men who are unable to trust in the goodness

It is time to face the music.

God, ever the just judge, questions them as to what has just transpired before handing down judgment. He begins with the man. "Who told you that you were naked? Have you eaten from the tree from which I commanded you not to eat?" (Gen. 3:11).

It's interesting that the man is the first to be questioned, when the woman was the one who took the first bite. Some have assumed that this shows God held Adam responsible for his wife. But remember, nothing in the first two chapters gives any indication of a hierarchy between them. It seems more likely Adam was first to be questioned, because he was the one who had received the prohibition directly from God. Firsthand knowledge is far more powerful than a second-hand account.

The deterioration of Adam and Eve's relationship now becomes even more apparent as Adam throws Eve under the bus. "The woman whom You gave to be with me, she gave me some of the fruit of the tree, and I ate" (v. 12). So much for oneness and mutual respect.

When God questions Eve, she in turn places the blame for her sin on Satan. "The serpent deceived me, and I ate" (v. 13). Neither one is willing to take responsibility for their actions.

What Judgment Did God Hand Down for Their Sin?

The testimonies have been heard. Now God begins to pronounce his judgment. First, Satan is cursed.

"Because you have done this, cursed are you more than all cattle, and more than every beast of the field; on your belly you will go, and dust you will eat all the days of your life." But there is a future, even greater penalty than having to slither along the ground. "I will put enmity between you and the woman and between your seed and her seed; He shall bruise you on the head, and you shall bruise Him on the heel" (3:14–15 NASB1995).

---

of God. Walter Brueggemann, *Genesis, Interpretation: A Bible Commentary for Teaching and Preaching* (Louisville, Kentucky: John Knox Press, 1982), 49.

The woman's *seed* is her offspring. One day, her descendant would deliver a fatal blow to Satan's dominion and power.

It's such a wonderful truth: just as soon as the first sin was committed, God promised a solution to its damaging existence. Jesus Christ, born of a woman, would fulfill this promise when he rose from the dead. It was just a matter of time; his emancipating victory over sin and death was already determined.

God then moves on to the woman. Notice how he begins his judgment: unlike the serpent, the woman is not cursed. In fact, *God does not curse either the woman or the man.* The curses are reserved for the serpent and the ground. So, because it is not designated as a curse, it seems Adam and Eve are rather being given a description of what their lives will be like in the wake of sin.

Both Adam and Eve receive similar pronouncements about their future lives. God describes how life has changed for both of them (3:16–17 NASB1995, emphasis mine).

> To Eve: "I will greatly multiply your *pain* in childbirth, in *pain* you will bring forth children."
> To Adam: "In *toil* you will eat of it [the ground] all the days of your life."

The original Hebrew word[4] translated here as *pain*[5] for Eve is the same word translated in the next verse as *toil* for Adam. (The fact gets lost in the English versions that the two different translations are from the same word.[6]) Sin has changed the quality of life for both of them, transforming their once toil-free existence into a lifelong struggle.

---

4. Alternate translations for the Hebrew word transliterated *'itstsabown* (determined by context): sorrow, toil, or hardship. Francis Brown, S. R. Driver, and Charles Briggs, *The Brown-Driver-Briggs Hebrew and English Lexicon* (Peabody, MA: Hendrickson, 2006), 781.
5. New American Standard Bible and most translations. The King James translates it as "sorrow." Both are possible meanings of this word.
6. The difference in understanding of this word contributes to the different ways of viewing how men and women interact today.

Eve's toil would be in having children, Adam's would be in laboring in the ground.

Nature would now work against them. This was a big change in their relationship to what they were originally given to dominate.

Another terrible consequence of sin was the change in their relationship with each other. Whereas before, they existed in harmony as one flesh, now there would be contention between them. God told Eve: "Your desire will be for your husband, and he shall rule over you" (v. 16).[7]

There is much discussion on what Eve's *desire* would entail. Is the woman's desire to control or dominate the man? Or is it a longing for the husband she had before the fall?

Many Hebrew lexicons define the word "desire" (*teshuqah*) along the lines of "longing" or "attract, impel of desire, affection."[8,9] This Hebrew word is used two other times in the Bible. In Genesis 4:7, when God is speaking to Cain, he says, "And if you do not do well, sin is lurking at the door; and its *desire* is for you, but you must master it" (emphasis mine). In this case, sin's desire is to take over, or dominate. But in Song of Solomon 7:10, desire comes across very differently: "I am my beloved's, and his *desire* is for me" (emphasis mine).

Context is critical to informing our ideas of what it means here in Genesis 3. It is the object of the desire that characterizes *teshuqah*. But no matter what Eve's desire means here, one thing is clear. It will never be fulfilled. Instead, their relationship will be marked with conflict.

---

7. There is some controversy over the meaning of "desire."
8. *The Brown-Driver-Briggs Hebrew and English Lexicon* also states that *teshuqah* is from the root *shuq*, which means "to run after, to desire, longing." Brown et al., *Hebrew and English Lexicon*, 1003.
9. Another context is available in the ancient Greek translation, the Septuagint. It used the word *apostrophe*, which was used in an extrabiblical source by Flavius Josephus to mean turning to someone for deliverance: "But still, because there appeared no other way whither they could turn themselves for deliverance (*apostrophe*), they made haste the same way with the soldiers, and went to Claudius." Josephus, *Josephus: The Complete Works*, trans. William Whiston (Nashville: Thomas Nelson, 1998), 733.

Before the fall, Adam and Eve's relationship was characterized by harmony and oneness.[10] From now on, Adam will dominate or rule over her, putting them into direct contention with each other. As Bruce Waltke wrote, "Control has replaced freedom; coercion has replaced persuasion; division has replaced multiplication."[11] The beautiful relationship has been perverted, which is what sin always does. It warps God's perfect creation.

Was God's Description for Eve a Mandate for All Time?

Should we understand what God says here as a command? That God's *design* is for the man to rule over the woman? Or is it instead a "horrifying consequence of humanity's fall into sin" and not the will of God at all?[12] In view of what Genesis 1–2 tells us, I suggest the latter. God's created order became hierarchical only after the fall and was not how he intended the relationship to be.

Hierarchy is a *perversion* of his original creation, not a God-ordained design.

In many evangelical circles, Genesis 3:16 has long been held to prove a God-designed hierarchy between woman and man. But after carefully examining the text, I am not convinced.

The fallacy of thinking of God's description after the fall as a *rule* to be obeyed for all time is evidenced in the ways such an interpretation has been enforced in the real world. When that interpretation is carried out to its full, what you get is nothing short of ridiculous.

Take, for example, what God said to Eve about the toil of childbirth. In 1591, the distinguished noblewoman Lady Eufame Macalyene asked for pain relief from her midwife during labor. The midwife reported this to the church authorities, who arrested the young mother. She was found guilty of violating "the doctrine of the primeval curse on women."[13] She was burned alive for her terrible crime.

---

10. See pages 25–27 in chapter 1 for notes on oneness.
11. Bruce J. Waltke, *Genesis: A Commentary* (Grand Rapids: Zondervan, 2001), 94.
12. Helga and Bob Edwards, *Equality Workbook: Freedom in Christ from the Oppression of Patriarchy* (self-pub., CreateSpace, 2016), 15.
13. Robert W. Winters, MD, *Accidental Medical Discoveries: How Tenacity and Pure*

Even by the 1800s, most people believed that while the use of pain relief was fine for surgery, it was not for childbirth. Many continued to think experiencing pain in childbirth was a woman's religious duty.[14] Today, this belief is almost universally rejected.

We have unashamedly made great strides in alleviating the toil of humankind that came into existence after the fall. Farm equipment and chemical control of weeds make it possible to produce a bountiful harvest and greatly reduces the toil of agriculture. Women are routinely given drugs or employ labor techniques to minimize their discomfort in childbirth. Today, no one blinks an eye at Christians taking advantage of these breakthroughs. No one considers this to be disobedience to God's "command."

It is a case of endorsing one "rule" and not others. Why arbitrarily decide that while two of God's pronouncements can be overcome, men ruling over women should remain? Shouldn't it be an all-or-nothing kind of thing? We cannot separate one out of the bunch then delight in alleviating the others. It's absolutely inconsistent.

But if God was *describing* the effects of sin, we can legitimately take pleasure in the advances that have been made over the centuries. We can correctly consider them redemption from the effects of sin, not disobedience to a rule.

To base our relationships on a result of turning away from God makes no sense. We have been set free from that destructive path, free to follow in Jesus's footsteps, free to pursue him in all ways. Including how we relate to each other.

There are other passages in the New Testament often used to interpret the Genesis creation and fall accounts (see 1 Tim. 2:11–15; 1 Cor. 11:8–9; Rom. 5:12–18; 2 Cor. 11:3). We will examine these in subsequent chapters. But we first need to look at each passage within its own context, to determine how its first readers would have

---

Dumb Luck Changed the World (New York: Skyhorse Publishing, 2016), 22.

14. Randi Hutter Epstein, MD, *Get Me Out: A History of Childbirth from the Garden of Eden to the Sperm Bank* (New York: W. W. Norton & Company, Inc., 2010).

understood it. It is only then we can be sure of the original intended meaning and find the principle it expresses. This is crucial before using one passage to interpret another.

Good News for Today

In the fall, all creation was tainted by sin. That includes the relationship between men and women. No longer did they perfectly reflect the glory of God. As Paul wrote to the Romans, "For all have sinned and *fall short of the glory of God*" (Rom. 3:23, emphasis mine).

It was a hopeless situation, until Jesus went to the cross. His sacrifice paid for the sin of the world (see 1 John 2:2). It changed everything: "Now the Lord is the Spirit, and where the Spirit of the Lord is, there is freedom" (2 Cor. 3:17).

Jesus's sacrificial work on the cross has allowed us to break free of sin's hold on us. "Our old self was crucified with Him, in order that our body of sin might be done away with, so that we would no longer be slaves to sin; for the one who has died is freed from sin. . . . For sin shall not be master over you, for you are not under the Law but under grace" (Rom. 6:6–7, 14).

Jesus has set us free. We can overcome the consequences of sin, because, in a believer, sin no longer reigns. Husbands and wives can now have the kind of relationship God originally designed for them. Harmonious. Equally suited to reflect God's image. To truly function as one.

Because of Jesus, we have a new potential to reverse the effects of sin in the marriage relationship. Whereas just after the fall, control replaced freedom, now, post-cross, freedom can replace control. What was perverted under sin's domination is ruled by it no more.

The Holy Spirit indwelled us at the moment of our salvation. The evidence of his presence is love, joy, peace, patience, kindness, goodness, faithfulness, gentleness, and self-control (see Gal. 5:22–23). God's ultimate intent for us is to be conformed to the image of Jesus Christ (see Rom. 8:29). "But we all, with unveiled faces, looking as in a mirror at the glory of the Lord, are being transformed into the same image from glory to glory, just as from the Lord, the Spirit" (2 Cor. 3:18).

As he transforms us, our relationships will be transformed as well. We will be motivated to unconditionally love each other because of the great love he has for us. We will be inclined to give grace to each other because of the abundant grace he has granted us, both in our salvation and our continuing relationship with him.

When Paul urged the Ephesians to yield to the Spirit, he qualified what that would look like in a marriage relationship: submitting to one another in the fear of Christ (see Eph. 5:18, 21).[15] What once was characterized by an uneven distribution of power will be transformed into mutual submission.

How does that happen?

What God describes in Genesis 3 is a relationship battleground: two people with different agendas and values, endlessly striving for what they think they need. When in a relationship with Jesus, we start to look beyond ourselves, and our greatest desire is to live for him.

Before an orchestra performance, all instruments need to be tuned. To accomplish that, every instrument is made to match a common frequency. That note is provided by the oboe, because that instrument's pitch stands out and is steadier than that of other instruments. Without that common pitch, all instruments will remain hopelessly out of tune with each other. The resulting performance would be more noise than music. But when everyone is tuned to a common source outside of themselves, the sound produced when the conductor flicks her baton and the performance begins is absolutely beautiful.

When a husband and wife are tuned in to the same God, the One outside of themselves, they will be able to get out of their own heads and into the mind of Christ. It will be his kind of love that they will share: putting their spouse's needs above their own. The potential for

---

15. "Be filled with the Spirit . . . subject yourselves to one another in the fear of Christ." (We will cover this passage in greater detail in chapter 9.)

a conflict of interest is reduced dramatically, as each is now about the other rather than for himself or herself.

Only when both spouses are ready to give up their agenda for the sake of Christ can they enact the kind of mutual submission Paul is talking about in Ephesians. And when they do, their relationship will reflect what they were originally created to be: harmonious, loving with sacrificial love, and truly functioning as one. We can overcome the effects of sin cited by God in Genesis 3 through Christ's work on the cross. We have been set free.

Chapter 3

Does God Approve of Women Leading?

Then the sons of Israel again did evil in the sight of the LORD, after Ehud died. So the LORD sold them into the hand of Jabin king of Canaan, who reigned in Hazor; and the commander of his army was Sisera, who lived in Harosheth-hagoyim. The sons of Israel cried out to the LORD; for he had nine hundred iron chariots, and he oppressed the sons of Israel severely for twenty years.

Now Deborah, a prophetess, the wife of Lappidoth, was judging Israel at that time. She used to sit under the palm tree of Deborah between Ramah and Bethel in the hill country of Ephraim; and the sons of Israel went up to her for judgment. Now she sent word and summoned Barak the son of Abinoam from Kedesh-naphtali, and said to him, "The LORD, the God of Israel, has indeed commanded, 'Go and march to Mount Tabor, and take with you ten thousand men from the sons of Naphtali and from the sons of Zebulun. I will draw out to you Sisera, the commander of Jabin's army, with his chariots and his many troops to the river Kishon, and I will hand him over to you.'" Then Barak said to her, "If you will go with me, then I will go; but if you will not go with me, I will not go." She said, "I will certainly go with you; however, the fame shall not be yours on the journey that you are about to take, for the LORD will sell Sisera into the hand of a woman." Then Deborah got up and went with Barak to Kedesh. Barak summoned Zebulun and Naphtali to

Kedesh, and ten thousand men went up with him; Deborah also went up with him.

Now Heber the Kenite had separated himself from the Kenites, from the sons of Hobab the father-in-law of Moses, and had pitched his tent as far away as the oak in Zaanannim, which is near Kedesh.

Then they told Sisera that Barak the son of Abinoam had gone up to Mount Tabor. Sisera summoned all his chariots, nine hundred iron chariots, and all the people who were with him, from Harosheth-hagoyim to the river Kishon. Then Deborah said to Barak, "Arise! For this is the day on which the LORD has handed Sisera over to you; behold, the LORD has gone out before you." So Barak went down from Mount Tabor with ten thousand men following him. And the LORD routed Sisera and all his chariots and all his army with the edge of the sword before Barak; and Sisera got down from his chariot and fled on foot. But Barak pursued the chariots and the army as far as Harosheth-hagoyim, and all the army of Sisera fell by the edge of the sword; not even one was left.

Now Sisera fled on foot to the tent of Jael the wife of Heber the Kenite, because there was peace between Jabin the king of Hazor and the house of Heber the Kenite. And Jael went out to meet Sisera, and said to him, "Turn aside, my master, turn aside to me! Do not be afraid." So he turned aside to her into the tent, and she covered him with a rug. And he said to her, "Please give me a little water to drink, for I am thirsty." So she opened a leather bottle of milk and gave him a drink; then she covered him. And he said to her, "Stand in the doorway of the tent, and it shall be if anyone comes and inquires of you, and says, 'Is there anyone here?' that you shall say, 'No.'" But Jael, Heber's wife, took a tent peg and a hammer in her hand, and went secretly to him and drove the peg into his temple, and it went through into the ground; for he was sound asleep and exhausted. So he died. And behold, while Barak was pursuing Sisera, Jael came out to meet him and said to him, "Come, and I will show you the man whom you are seeking." So he entered with her, and behold, Sisera was lying dead with the tent peg in his temple.

So God subdued Jabin the king of Canaan on that day before the sons of Israel. And the hand of the sons of Israel pressed harder and harder upon Jabin the king of Canaan, until they had eliminated Jabin the king of Canaan.

—Judges 4

Focus on Judges 4–5

The summer I graduated from college, an announcement was given at church on several consecutive Sundays: there was a desperate need for a new Sunday school superintendent. Concerned at the obvious lack of volunteers, I finally approached an elder. I had just received a degree in elementary education. I knew I was still green as an educator, but I thought I probably knew more about a classroom than the average person. At the very least, educating children was my passion. And a young girl like me was better than no one. I offered to take on the responsibility.

I could see from the look on my elder's face that I had just suggested the impossible. He kindly sat down to show me from Scripture why it was inappropriate for a woman ever to lead a ministry that involved men. As discouraging as it was, I did not question his gentle instruction at the time. He had a verse for everything, after all.

I loved the Lord with all my heart and wanted to do what his Word said. But as much as I felt I should rest in my church leaders' wisdom, a nagging question remained for me: *What about Deborah? Didn't she lead?*

A few years later, I asked a preacher about the Old Testament account of Deborah. He assured me: God had merely made an exception to his rule. He was forced to, since there were no men qualified to lead at that time. He really wanted to use a man, but all he could find was a woman. So a woman was called, but only for that specific, unusual time.

His view of God was shocking to me. God couldn't have had the right man in place for the job? The preacher was depicting God as helpless in the face of certain circumstances, forced to contradict his own standard.[1] Couldn't God see ahead and plan accordingly? Wasn't God more powerful than that? It was a very limiting view of God.

And there were the other women who had leadership roles in Scripture, both in the Old and New Testaments. The more of them I discovered, the more my doubt grew. What about Miriam, Moses's sister? What about Ruth? Esther? Rahab? Mary Magdalene? Priscilla? Each of them led by taking the initiative, moving forward at the Lord's leading. Men followed their lead and God blessed that obedience. How many "exceptions" did we need before accepting a woman leader as appropriate for any point in time?

We've already seen God's original intent and design for women at creation. We've also seen that after the fall, the relationship between man and woman changed. Their perfect harmony and oneness would be perverted into a power struggle. It was one of many consequences of the introduction of sin into the world.

But was God establishing a new rule with that proclamation? Or was he *describing* the change in their relationship? If it was a rule—the God-ordained way all women should interact with men—you would think he would never put a woman in charge. Why would he go against his own decree? Wouldn't that be directly leading that woman into sin?

That doesn't sound like God at all (see James 1:13).

There are many women in the Old Testament whose lives seem to defy a traditionally held prohibition of women leading men. In this chapter, we will take a close look at Deborah. Her story is an important part of the book of Judges, indicated by the amount of space the writer gives it. So, we will examine these chapters, in search of clues about God's view of female leadership, especially over men.

---

1. Assuming Deborah was chosen out of desperation because of the pressing situation at hand ignores the fact that Deborah had a leadership role long before calling Barak. She was judging and prophesying when she received a word from the Lord that redemption was imminent (see Judg. 4:4–7). Her people respected her. Barak and his army obeyed her command.

What Were the Circumstances When
Deborah Became Judge over Israel?

The story of this remarkable woman is set in the time period follow-ing the conquest of Canaan and settlement of the twelve tribes of Israel into the promised land. There was no king. Instead God went before them, empowering, guiding, and providing for his people.[2] But eventually, after that first generation died out, their children and children's children drifted away from the Lord, choosing to follow pagan gods.

Not a good move. God sent in enemies to oppress the nation as a repeated wake-up call. The Israelites struggled under fierce oppression for years. Finally, each time they would come to their senses and call on the one true God to rescue them. In response, he sent judges, one after another, who led them to victory over the oppressing kingdom, ousting the enemy from the land. Israel rejoiced at God's deliverance. But it wasn't long before they would turn back to their sin, following the gods of the Canaanites once more.

Disobedience, judgment, a cry for deliverance, and God's provi-sion of a judge to lead them out of oppression: the recurrent events of the book of Judges were a classic case of history repeating itself.[3] What a dismal picture of humankind's propensity to sin, in spite of having a perfect King over them.

Every God-appointed judge (there are twelve named in this book) was male—with one exception. In Judges 4, the writer introduces us to Deborah. This time around, the punishing enemy was Jabin, the king of Canaan. His was a strong military presence: his army had

---

2. In a few centuries, Israel would demand a human king. God's response? "They have rejected Me from being King over them" (1 Sam. 8:7).

3. Each new cycle begins with something similar to "Then the sons of Israel again did evil in the sight of the LORD" (see Judg. 2:11; 3:7; 4:1; 6:1; 10:6; 13:1). The narrator informs us: "Wherever they went, the hand of the LORD was against them for evil . . . so that they were severely distressed. Then the LORD raised up judges who saved them from the hands of those who plundered them . . . for the LORD was moved to pity by their groaning. . . . But it came about, when the judge died, that they would turn back and act more corruptly than their fathers" (Judg. 2:15–16, 18–19).

nine hundred iron chariots. Israel had no hope of victory over such military might. The severe occupation of their land had gone on for twenty long years. Jabin's chariots ruled the valleys. The main roads became so dangerous, merchants and farmers were forced to travel the smaller paths on the hillsides (see Judg. 5:6). Finally, the sons of Israel had had enough of living in fear. They cried out to the Lord for help.

And the Lord gave Israel Deborah.

What Significance Did Deborah's Dual Roles of Prophetess and Judge Have in Describing Deborah's Leadership in Israel?

The narrator introduces Deborah as a prophetess and a judge. The Hebrew term translated as *judge* is used for an individual who maintains justice for the tribes of Israel. But other than Samuel, who was the last (and seemingly greatest) judge, not one of the other judges is recorded as serving in the actual work of jurisprudence—with the exception of Deborah. We are told that the sons of Israel respected her wisdom and sought her out for arbitration.

Deborah held court under "The Palm Tree of Deborah," located between two cities in the hill country of the tribe of Ephraim.[4] This meeting place was located on an international trade and military route connecting Asia, Africa, and Europe.[5,6] The way her location is described in the text suggests her influence went far beyond a single tribe.[7]

Deborah refers to nine of the twelve tribes of Israel in her song in chapter 5. Her mention of so many tribes suggests that many of

---

4. Ephraim was the southernmost region of the future Northern Kingdom of Israel.
5. Ronald W. Pierce, "Deborah: Troublesome Woman or Woman of Valor?", *Priscilla Papers* 32, no. 2 (Spring 2018): 3.
6. Samuel the prophet later led from practically the same location (see 1 Sam. 7:15–16; 8:4).
7. In her song (Judges 5), Deborah references seven other tribes (outside of the two who went to battle). That would give her a territory that stretched from Israel's northwest coastal plain to the southern extremities of the Jordan River.

the tribes deferred to her counsel and rulings.[8] Each of the tribes was autonomous. No one tribe could tell any other tribe what to do.[9] But here in the narrative of chapter 4, Deborah commands the armies of two tribes into action.

Clearly, her influence as a leader went beyond leading the nation into battle. Her arbitration was respected and upheld.[10]

Deborah was also a prophetess. This means she received and delivered messages from God to the people. Prophets were authoritative, due to the origin of what they spoke.[11] There were people who prophesied who were not clearly identified as prophets in their time (for example, David), but in Judges, Deborah most certainly is.

Deborah spoke the Word of God authoritatively to the people. They deferred their legal matters to her in respect for her position, leadership, and assumedly, her character. Her dual roles as prophetess and judge demonstrate how critical her leadership role was to the daily affairs of the region.

Was Barak Wrong in Following Her Lead?

At some point in her position of authority, Deborah sent for Barak and told him, "The LORD, the God of Israel, has indeed commanded, 'Go and march to Mount Tabor, and take with you ten thousand men from the sons of Naphtali and from the sons of Zebulun'" (Judg.

---

8. Deborah's victory song is recorded in Judges chapter 5. Aside from Naphtali and Zebulun, those tribes named are Ephraim, Benjamin, and Manasseh, v. 14; Issachar and Reuben, v. 15; Dan and Asher, v. 17.

9. Judges 1:3 shows the tribe of Judah enlisting the help of the tribe of Simeon, who were operating independently until then. The first central government mentioned in Scripture is at the reign of Saul.

10. Deborah is also described as "a mother in Israel" (Judg. 5:7), who had the support of the "princes of Issachar" (Judg. 5:15), suggesting a matriarchal rule over the nation. Elijah is called father (2 Kings 2:12) as is Elisha (2 Kings 13:14), and so is an unnamed Levite who is being commissioned to be a spiritual guide for the nation (Judg. 17:7–10; 18:18–19).

11. As Amos wrote, "Certainly the Lord GOD does nothing unless He reveals His secret plan to His servants the prophets. A lion has roared! Who will not fear? The Lord GOD has spoken! Who can do anything but prophesy?" (Amos 3:7–8). Balaam the prophet said, "I will bring word back to you just as the LORD may speak to me" (Num. 22:8).

4:6).[12] Barak did not question the orders, but begged Deborah to go with him as he obeyed them, presumably so she could deliver further instruction from the Lord in the heat of the battle. His request indicates respect for her leadership and authenticity as from the Lord.

Deborah agrees to his request: "I will certainly go with you." But she also warns: "However, the fame shall not be yours on the journey that you are about to take, for the LORD will sell Sisera into the hand of a woman" (v. 9). The Lord would give them the victory, but personal glory would not be awarded to Barak.

He went in obedience anyway.

I've heard a lot of criticism about Barak over the years. That he was hiding behind a woman, too cowardly to face the battle on his own. But the *actual text* does not treat him as anything but obedient and humble.[13] He agreed immediately to Deborah's command and appropriately viewed it as from the Lord. He wasted no time in calling the troops and went into battle with confidence, trusting the Lord's promise that he would go before them.[14]

There is not one mention in Scripture of impropriety on the part of Deborah or Barak. God totally blessed them and used them in his plan to rescue Israel. Not one sign of his displeasure is recorded in the text or even implied.

Did God Indicate His Approval for Deborah's Leadership Position?

In trust and obedience to the word of the Lord, the armies of Naphtali and Zebulon rallied. They took up a strategic location on the high ground of Mt. Tabor, where the terrain prohibited Jabin's powerful chariots from engaging. His general, Sisera, heard of their gathering

---

12. This is another evidence of her leadership: giving a decisive command like this.
13. The NIV's unfortunate translation injects a rebuke into Deborah's warning, as a result of his request: "But *because of the course you are taking*, the honor will not be yours, for the LORD will deliver Sisera into the hands of a woman" (v. 9). The words in italic are not in the original Hebrew.
14. In the so-called Hebrews' "Hall of Faith," Barak is given only accolades. He is included in a list of men "who by faith conquered kingdoms, [and] performed acts of righteousness" (Heb. 11:32–33).

and ordered his army out to quash the uprising. Soon they arrived at the Jezreel Valley just below Barak's position. No doubt Sisera was confident in the strength of his army. But he didn't take one very important fact into account: the living, true God would go before Israel and give them the victory.

And that's exactly what happened. God created a sudden storm to cause the waters of the Kishon River to overflow their banks, turning the level, surrounding plain into a quagmire (see Judg. 5:21).[15] The heavy iron chariots were quickly bogged down in the mud.

It was time to strike. Deborah told Barak: "Arise! For this is the day on which the LORD has handed Sisera over to you; behold, the LORD has gone out before you" (Judg. 4:14). Barak gave the go-ahead signal to the waiting troops.

Ten thousand soldiers roared down the mountain. They may have been underequipped, but they went in the strength of the Lord. With their iron chariots incapacitated, the Canaanite army had been stopped dead in their tracks. There was no question as to who had the upper hand. Sisera and his army were about to be routed.

General Sisera could see the imminent defeat. Rather than stay with his troops until the end, he surreptitiously bailed. Judges tells us his entire army fell by the edge of the sword; not even one was left . . . except for Sisera.

But the final word had not yet been spoken. Spotting the camp of a known ally, Sisera ducked into the tent of Jael, the wife of Heber the Kenite. Jael covered him with a rug, feigning an intention to hide him from his enemies. She calmed him down, gave him milk to slake his extreme thirst, and waited until he fell asleep from exhaustion. Then

---

15. This scenario was miraculous in its timing. Deborah notes, "The earth quaked [because of thunder?], the heavens also dripped," indicating a storm sent just at the right time by the Lord to inundate the valley with a sudden flood (Judg. 5:4). "In Palestine, the pleasant, bone-dry valley of summertime frequently becomes an angry, turbulent flood that demolishes everything in its path during the winter rains." Ronald F. Youngblood, "WADI" in *Nelson's New Illustrated Bible Dictionary*, ed. F. F. Bruce and R. K. Harrison (Nashville: Thomas Nelson, 1995), 1298.

she picked up a tent peg and a hammer and drove the peg right through his temple and into the ground. The last enemy soldier had fallen.

Barak, in hot pursuit of Sisera, finally arrived. Jael brought him into her tent and showed him the lifeless body of the enemy general. Everything had happened exactly as it had been foretold by Deborah.

Meanwhile, Israel continued routing the enemy out of the land until they were completely destroyed. God had used two women to play the key roles in his rescue of the nation. This story gives us real insight into his heart and purposes for women.

Good News for Today

It has always been God's plan to establish his kingdom on earth—a kingdom that values the leadership of both men and women. We see early indications of this through many examples in the Old Testament. Even in those ancient, strictly patriarchal societies, God used women in prominent ways.

Before Deborah lived, there were two women noted for prominence in the faith (listed as such in the book of Hebrews): Sarah and Rahab (see Heb. 11:11–21, 31).[16] Also before Deborah, Miriam, the older sister of Moses, had a leadership role over Israel in the wilderness (see Exod. 15:20–21; Num. 12:1–15, Mic. 6:4).[17]

After Deborah, the leaders of Israel went to Huldah the prophetess for guidance from the Lord (see 2 Kings 22:14–20; 2 Chron. 34:22–28). King Josiah showed his trust in what she told them by initiating a revival. Queen Esther became the hero of the Jews in exile when God used her to rescue a nation. In celebration of this event, the days of Purim were established as a national holiday at her command (see Esther 4:14–16; 9:29–32).

The Old Testament prophet Joel foretold of a time when God would pour his Spirit on humankind, specifically "your sons *and*

---

16. Rahab's story can be found in Joshua 2 and 6:23–25. She is also named in the genealogy of Jesus in Matt. 1:5 and in James 2:25.
17. The prophet Micah named Miriam right alongside her brothers Moses and Aaron in leadership (see Mic. 6:4).

daughters will prophesy. . . . Even on the male *and female* servants I will pour out My Spirit in those days" (Joel 2:28–29, emphasis mine). Kingdom values were further revealed just before Jesus's birth in Mary's burst of praise: "He has done mighty deeds with His arm; He has scattered those who were proud in the thoughts of their hearts. He has brought down rulers from their thrones, and has *exalted those who were humble.* He has filled the hungry with good things, and sent away the rich empty-handed" (Luke 1:51–53, emphasis mine). Women were definitely a part of "the oppressed" at the time of Jesus's birth.[18] The soon-to-be-born Messiah would come to set them free.

When Jesus came to earth, part of his earthly ministry was teaching about the coming kingdom of God (Mark 1:14–15). He described it as an unusual kingdom, set apart from all others. Its king would have an eternal reign. Its subjects would serve rather than expect to be served. In any human society, the strong hold the power and are assigned the greatest value. But God's kingdom would be far removed from the norm: the last would be first, and the first would be last. God would use the "foolish" to shame the wise. It would be an upside-down kingdom, at least according to the world, fully exemplifying the values of God.

Jesus personified those kingdom values. While living in a patriarchal society, he went against societal norms by scandalously including women in his traveling entourage of disciples (see Luke 8:1–3).[19] He commended Mary of Bethany (Martha's sister) for sitting at his feet and listening intently to his teaching, at a time

---

18. In a Hellenistic-influenced society, women were considered less than. Aristotle wrote, "We should look upon the female state of being as though it were a deformity, though on which occurs in the ordinary course of nature." Aristotle, *Metaphysics*, quoted in Rosalind Miles, *The Women's History of the World* (Topsfield, MA: Salem House, 1989), 57. A woman could not travel without permission from her husband. She did not receive a formal education. She was expected to remain at home to raise children and was banned from taking part in much of public life.

19. Craig S. Keener, *The IVP Bible Background Commentary: New Testament* (Downers Grove, IL: InterVarsity Press, 1993), 209–10.

when that kind of discussion typically excluded women (see Luke 10:38–42).[20]

There are ten personal conversations between Jesus and women recorded in the Gospels. These women were from many different walks of life and presented very different needs. But no matter who they were or what they needed, when they encountered Jesus, he was all in. Each woman had his complete attention, even when surrounded by a crowd.

After Jesus's resurrection, Mary Magdalene was the first person to whom Jesus appeared. He gave her the responsibility of informing the rest of the disciples that he had risen. This was at a time when a woman's testimony in court was ruled invalid because of her gender.[21]

Through the way he lived his life on earth, Jesus made his message clear: in God's kingdom, women matter.

In the book of Acts, at Pentecost, Peter declared that God's Spirit had been poured out on the group of believers with him. He acknowledged this as a fulfillment of Joel's prophecy, that both sons and daughters of God would prophesy, spreading the gospel news to the world (see Acts 2:14–21).

Paul wrote the Philippians that all believers are citizens of God's kingdom. "For our citizenship is in heaven, from which we also eagerly wait for a Savior, the Lord Jesus Christ; who will transform the body of our lowly condition into conformity with His glorious body, by the exertion of the power that He has even to subject all things to Himself" (Phil. 3:20–21).

Citizens of the kingdom of God live with an eye toward the day when their heavenly kingdom will be consummated on earth, as Jesus comes back to reign. To think like a citizen of the kingdom, we must look back to God's intentions for humans before the fall distorted it all.

Why? Jesus has released us from the power of sin, including the power of sin in our relationships. No longer must we live in a hierarchy

---

20. Keener, *IVP*, 218.
21. Keener, *IVP*, 316.

between man and woman created by the introduction of sin into the world. We can live our lives in harmony once again, because Jesus's work on the cross has set us free.

Until Jesus returns, we are representatives of heaven to a world still under the power of sin. One way to reflect the reality of God's kingdom is to have healthy marriages and relationships within the church. This includes women leading, just as they were created to do in Genesis 1:28. Just as it was *before* sin.

Does God approve of women leading? Through Deborah's story and other Old and New Testament examples shining through the dark veil of sin's effect, God has demonstrated the value he places on women and his intention to use them in a variety of leadership roles.

Chapter 4

Did Jesus View Women as Second-Class Citizens?

Soon afterward, Jesus began going around from one city and village to another, proclaiming and preaching the kingdom of God. The twelve were with Him, and also some women who had been healed of evil spirits and sicknesses: Mary who was called Magdalene, from whom seven demons had gone out, and Joanna the wife of Chuza, Herod's steward, and Susanna, and many others who were contributing to their support out of their private means.

—Luke 8:1–3

Now as they were traveling along, He entered a village; and a woman named Martha welcomed Him into her home. And she had a sister called Mary, who was also seated at the Lord's feet, and was listening to His word.

—Luke 10:38–39

Now the women who had come with Him from Galilee followed, and they saw the tomb and how His body was laid. And then they returned and prepared spices and perfumes.

And on the Sabbath they rested according to the commandment.

But on the first day of the week, at early dawn, they came to the tomb bringing the spices which they had prepared. And they found the stone rolled away from the tomb, but when they entered, they did not find the body of the Lord Jesus. While they were perplexed about this, behold, two men suddenly stood near them in gleaming clothing; and as the women were terrified and bowed their faces to the ground, the men said to them, "Why are you seeking the living One among the dead? He is not here, but He has risen. Remember how He spoke to you while He was still in Galilee, saying that the Son of Man must be handed over to sinful men, and be crucified, and on the third day rise from the dead." And they remembered His words, and returned from the tomb and reported all these things to the eleven, and to all the rest.

—Luke 23:55–24:9

Focus on Matthew, Mark, Luke, and John

As I entered The Well to begin teaching a new round of classes, I was greeted by many familiar faces. (Steve and I both teach at this non-profit organization that ministers to women in inner-city Baltimore.) But there was one woman I did not recognize. She was working behind the reception desk, glowing, full of enthusiasm and love.

As I signed in, she told me, "I've been waiting to meet you. We studied your book on Jesus and women last fall, and it changed my whole relationship with God. I always thought God didn't like women very much," she confessed. "But after reading the stories in your book, I know that is just not true."

As much as it meant to me to hear that God had used my words to draw her to him, I also felt grief for her former pain, because I, too, had struggled with the same tragic misunderstanding. As a youth, I knew God loved me but had observed there were two classes of individuals in his kingdom: men were the leaders, women were the followers. Did God love women less?

It's actually the reason I wrote my previous book, *Unexpected Love.* I wanted to find out once and for all what God really thought about women. Since Jesus was God in the flesh, it stood to reason I could discern God's heart through the conversations Jesus had with women in the Gospels. I was excited about what I would discover.

I started with the conversation Jesus had with his mother at the wedding in Cana. She had informed him that the host was out of wine. "Woman, what does that have to do with us?" he demanded (John 2:4 NASB1995). Commentators seemed to think he was putting Mary in her place. Not what I was hoping for. So I moved on to the next story, when Jesus encountered the Syrophoenician woman begging him to rid her daughter of demon possession. Jesus first ignored her, then finally responded by comparing her to the dogs that ate the crumbs under the master's table. Again, his response to her was disconcerting—and my anticipation began to turn to discouragement.

Story after story, Jesus seemed to treat women as less than, speaking careless and even hurtful words to women who were desperate or hurting. It was enough to give me second thoughts about writing that book.

But after my time in seminary, I knew a superficial read could lead to false impressions and a resulting bad interpretation. So I started over. One by one, I examined each passage with my training: translating from the original language, researching the cultural standards of the time, noticing where each Gospel writer placed the stories in terms of context. All the while, I prayed, asking God to clear my mind of any incorrect thinking or assumptions, in hopes that the Holy Spirit would lead me to the truths he wanted me to write.

I wasn't disappointed.

What slowly emerged as I worked was a radically different Savior than my initial readings had offered. Each woman Jesus encountered *mattered* to him. He gave them his intense, undivided attention. He met every one of them right where they were, saying exactly what they needed to hear, and did for them what needed to be done, all the while leading them into a deeper relationship with him. He was so very personal.

The more I studied, the deeper I fell in love with him.

Because the first-century church was founded mostly by Jews, Jewish attitudes toward women and Jesus's view of women are important contexts when studying Jesus's interactions with them. This chapter and the next will take a format different from the rest of this book, in that we will not explore a single passage. Instead, we will be aiming toward a birds-eye view, more survey than a verse-by-verse study. Our goal in this chapter is to discover Jesus's general attitude toward women.

How Were Women Generally Treated in Jesus's Day?

A woman in the first century lacked many of the freedoms women enjoy today. These restrictions came down from the top; the oral law that the Pharisees and scribes promoted was strict and demeaning toward females.[1]

By the beginning of the first century, the patriarchal culture we see in parts of the Old Testament had hardened into a stance that considered women as secondary to men.[2] We can see the reality of this in the compositions of first-century writers: according to Josephus, "The woman is inferior . . . to the man in every way."[3] Later, in the Talmud,[4] women were frequently classed with children and slaves.[5] Every morning, Jewish men recited the *Shema*, which included an expression of gratitude that they had not been created female.[6] It was generally held that women had been created unequal to men physically, socially, and ethically.

In court, testimony from a woman was not legally accepted.

Men largely held women responsible for the evil in the world, especially sexual sin. Philo wrote: "The attitude of man is informed by reason, that of woman by sensuality."[7] Because of women's assumed promiscuity, men were to avoid talking with them in public, lest she tempt them to sin. Rabbi Jose ben Johanan warned: "He that talks much with women brings evil upon himself."[8]

---

1. The oral law, they thought, guarded the people from sin. Rabbis of Jesus's day continued many old traditions and produced new ones which they thought would guard people from committing sin.
2. James B. Hurley, *Man and Woman in Biblical Perspective* (Grand Rapids: Zondervan, 1981), 73.
3. Hurley, *Man and Woman*, 61.
4. The Talmud is a written version of the oral law, and includes commentaries on it. It was written over the period between AD 100 and 400.
5. Hurley, *Man and Woman*, 62. He quotes Rabbi Aha ben Jacob, who wrote, "who hast not made me a slave. And is this not the same as a woman?" (bMen. 43a).
6. Rabbi Judah ben Elai, AD 150. bMen. 43b.
7. Philo, "De Opificio Mundi," in *Theological Dictionary of the New Testament,* vol. 1, ed. Gerhard Kittel and Gerhard Friedrich (Grand Rapids: Eerdmans, 1965), 782. Philo made it clear in his writings that he viewed the female as mentally inferior, selfish, and given to seduction.
8. Hurley, *Man and Woman*, 65.

Women were also overlooked when it came to religious matters. They were considered unteachable.[9] Rabbi Eliezer made a strong statement: "'If any man gives his daughter a knowledge of the Law, it is as though he taught her lechery' (m.Sotah 3:4)."[10] In the temple, women were restricted to the outer courts, leaving the innermost places to the men.[11] In the synagogue, they were frequently seated in a separate section from the men and not allowed to verbally participate.[12] It was considered inappropriate for a woman to study under a rabbi.[13]

But Jesus came to set them free.

What Did Jesus Teach That Challenged Those Pharisaical Teachings?

Jesus spent much of his earthly ministry teaching about the kingdom of God. There was a lot of damage to undo. In the previous centuries, the Pharisees had transformed Judaism into something it was never intended to be with their detailed oral law.[14] Life as a Jew had become all about works and external behavior, instead of a love for God (see Rom. 9:30–33).

Ironically, an external checklist was never the intent of Mosaic law. Just before they entered the promised land, God warned that superficial obedience was not what he wanted from his people. "And now, Israel, what does the LORD your God require of you, but to fear the LORD your God, to walk in all His ways and *love Him*, and to serve the LORD your God with *all your heart and with all your soul. . . . Circumcise your heart*, and do not stiffen your neck any longer.

---

9. Alice Mathews, *Gender Roles and the People of God: Rethinking What We Were Taught about Men and Women in the Church* (Grand Rapids: Zondervan, 2017), 51.
10. Mathews, *Gender Roles*, 71.
11. Hurley, *Man and Woman*, 71.
12. Hurley, *Man and Woman*, 73.
13. John Temple Bristow, *What Paul Really Said about Women* (San Francisco: HarperCollins, 1991), 34.
14. For example, there were over 1,000 commands on how one must keep the Sabbath alone!

. . . You shall fear the LORD your God; you shall serve Him, and *cling to Him,* and you shall swear by His name" (Deut. 10:12, 16, 20, emphasis mine).[15] God wanted something beyond following rules. He wanted their hearts.

Early in his ministry, Jesus revealed with his Sermon on the Mount just how misguided things had gotten. "You have heard that it was said . . ." he told his listeners, reminding them of the familiar Pharisaical interpretation of Mosaic law. "But *I* say to you . . ."[16] Jesus was opening his disciples' eyes to how off track their religion (and following the Mosaic law) had become. He was bringing their relationship with God right back to the heart.

When Jesus spoke at his hometown synagogue, he revealed one of Isaiah's messianic prophecies that he had come to fulfill: "The Spirit of the LORD is upon Me, because He anointed Me to preach the gospel to the poor. He has sent Me to proclaim release to the captive, and recovery of sight to the blind, to set free those who are oppressed, to proclaim the favorable year of the LORD" (Luke 4:18–19 NASB1995). Those less fortunate individuals (the poor, the captive, the blind, the oppressed) may have been insignificant to respectable society, but they mattered very much to God.[17]

Most Jews assumed the lower stratum of society suffered as a punishment for sin. It stood to reason, then, that those in power or of wealthy means were to be deemed especially spiritual, blessed by

---

15. Circumcision marked God's people as his. It was an outward sign of an inward committed relationship. God was asking them to "mark" their hearts, to match the internal to the external.

16. During the time period between the Old and New Testaments, Pharisees developed an oral law explaining how the 613 Mosaic Laws in the Torah were to be carried out. (These instructions were eventually recorded in the second century AD as the *Mishnah.*) But in their attempts to meet the letter of the Law, they lost the heart of the Law. In his Sermon on the Mount, in Matthew 5–7, Jesus is bringing people back to the full implications of God's Laws and away from the legalism that existed in his day.

17. The less fortunate always did matter to God: Mosaic law made provision for the infirm and the poor. See Exod. 22:22; 23:6, 11; Lev. 19:10; 23:22. There are many more commands in the Old Testament that reflect God's care for the disadvantaged.

God because of their righteous lives. It was a false spiritual hierarchy within the people of God, one that was judged by their station in life as well as a public obedience to the oral law.

A great example of this was when Jesus and his disciples came upon a man blind from birth. The disciples expressed their faulty assumption: "Rabbi, who sinned, this man or his parents, that he would be born blind?"

Jesus's answer turned their assumption upside down. "It was neither that this man sinned, nor his parents; but it was so that the works of God might be displayed in him" (John 9:2–3).

Jesus also turned common assumptions about leadership on their head. When the disciples asked who among them would be the greatest, he gave them shocking news: "The kings of the Gentiles domineer over them; and those who have authority over them are called 'Benefactors.' But *it is not this way for you*; rather, the one who is the greatest among you must become like the youngest, and the leader like the servant. For who is [presently seen as] greater, the one who reclines at the table or the one who serves? Is it not the one who reclines at the table? But I am among you as the one who serves" (Luke 22:25–27, emphasis mine). The greatest in God's kingdom would walk in the footsteps of Jesus and be the servants of all.

When parents brought their children to Jesus, his disciples rebuked them. But Jesus indignantly told them: "Allow the children to come to Me; do not forbid them; for the kingdom of God belongs to such as these." Then he added, "Truly I say to you, whoever does not receive the kingdom of God like a child will not enter it at all" (Mark 10:14–15). Children were weak and lived at the mercy of those who ruled over them. They had nothing to offer except obedient trust. Jesus knew that the proud or the confident would not see a need for a Savior. In their minds, they were on track, working their way into heaven.

But they would fail. Only the salvation God provided through his Son's death on the cross would clear the way to heaven. It was through faith alone and by grace alone that they could be saved.

When Jesus gave his Sermon on the Mount, he began with the Beatitudes, characterizing those who were citizens of the kingdom. Only those who understood they were poor in their spirit, who mourned their sin, and who looked to God alone for righteousness would be blessed. Jesus later told the scribes and Pharisees, "It is not those who are healthy who need a physician, but those who are sick; I did not come to call the [self-]righteous, but sinners [who understand just how needy they are]" (Mark 2:17).

On the night of the Last Supper, Jesus washed each disciple's feet (even Judas, whom he knew would betray him). Peter, still not grasping kingdom values, was horrified. "Never shall You wash my feet!" he exclaimed (John 13:8).

But Jesus answered, "You call Me 'Teacher' and 'Lord'; and you are right, for so I am. So if I, the Lord and the Teacher, washed your feet, you also ought to wash one another's feet. For I gave you an example, so that you also would do just as I did for you" (John 13:13–15). With that one act, Jesus denounced their assumptions about power and dominance. He would further reverse ideas of status and power with his death on the cross. His followers could not expect personal gain from their dedicated discipleship. They followed a suffering, humble Savior, who was obedient to the will of the Father even to his own death.

The kingdom of God is often aptly called "The Upside-Down Kingdom." Jesus's teachings certainly challenged the present order of his day. It was a total reversal of culturally accepted norms and urged his listeners toward humility.

How Did Jesus Interact with Women?

While the Pharisees kept women from being serious students of the Word, this was not God's plan for his kingdom. Back when the children of Israel first inhabited the promised land, every seven years they were to "assemble the people, the men, and *the women, the children,* and *the stranger* who is in your town, so that they may hear [the law read] and learn and fear the LORD your God, and be careful to follow all the words of this Law" (Deut. 31:12, emphasis mine). Consistent with kingdom values, God wanted women, children, and even Gentiles to hear his Word and trust in him.

Some fifteen hundred years later, Jesus was every bit as inclusive in his instruction. He welcomed the children with loving arms (see Mark 10:13–16). He miraculously fed four thousand people in Gentile territory (see Mark 8:1–10). He set the daughter of the Syrophoenician woman free from the demon that tormented her (see Mark 7:24–30). When a Roman centurion asked him to heal his beloved servant, Jesus healed him from afar (see Luke 7:2–10). He talked theology with a Samaritan woman at the well, revealing things about himself he had not yet revealed to anyone, not even his disciples (see John 4:7–30). There were no racial barriers with Jesus.

There were no gender barriers, either. He didn't hesitate to teach women as the Jewish leaders had. While visiting her home, Jesus welcomed Mary of Bethany to sit at his feet (a common posture for a rabbi's disciple) and discuss Scriptures with the men (see Luke 10:38–42).[18] He revealed that he was the Messiah openly for the first time to the Samaritan woman (see John 4:25–26). Outside her brother Lazarus's tomb, Martha was the first to hear Jesus call himself the Resurrection and the Life (see John 11:25–27). In response, Martha proclaimed her belief that he was the Messiah and the Son of God.

In fact, from what is recorded in the Gospels, some of the longest and deepest conversations Jesus had were with women.

Jesus scandalously included women in his entourage. Three of them were even named by Luke, identified as having traveled with Jesus since his early ministry in Galilee (see Luke 8:1–3). These were women completely dedicated to their Lord. They supported him with their private funds, listened to him teach, and watched him perform many miracles. They continued to follow him after his arrest and

---

18. To sit at the feet of a rabbi was synonymous with becoming his disciple. Kenneth E. Bailey, "Women in the New Testament: A Middle Eastern Cultural View," *Anglican Evangelical Journal for Theology and Mission* 6, no. 1 (January/February 2000): 2.

trials and stood by as he was nailed to the cross (see Luke 23:27–31; John 19:25). They stayed until the end, witnessing his excruciating death, and followed Joseph of Arimathea and Nicodemus to his burial place (see Luke 23:50–56).

After the Sabbath, those same women went to the tomb to be sure Jesus's body had been properly prepared for burial. As they listened to the angels recalling what Jesus had taught them about rising from the dead, they remembered Jesus's teaching (even when none of the remaining eleven disciples did; see Luke 24:1–9).

Who was the first to see the resurrected Jesus revealed? A woman, Mary Magdalene. Jesus gave her the assignment to announce to his disciples that he was alive (see John 20:17). They wouldn't believe her (Luke 24:11). But he sent her anyway.

Counter to the accepted attitudes toward women in his day, Jesus treated women with love and respect. They were important to him and important to the work of the kingdom.

Why Did Jesus Only Call Twelve Men to Be Disciples?

Back in Genesis, the grandson of Abraham (who was called into a special relationship with God, along with his future descendants), Jacob, had twelve sons. Those sons and their offspring became the tribes of Israel, and together would become the nation of Israel.

Many hundreds of years later, a civil war split the nation. The Northern Kingdom, called Israel, contained ten of the tribes. The Southern Kingdom was called Judah (which also contained the tribe of Benjamin). After completely failing to serve the Lord for 200 years, God used the Assyrian army in judgment to conquer Israel. Judah had its good moments, but eventually fell under judgment 137 years later to the Babylonians. Both kingdoms were carried off into exile after being conquered.

But God had not forgotten his people. He sent prophets during that exile to give people hope. Isaiah and Ezekiel foretold of a time when God would bring the scattered people back into the land. "Behold, I am going to take the sons of Israel from among the nations where they have gone, and I will gather them from every side and bring them into their own land; and I will make them one nation in the land, on the mountains of Israel; and one king will be king for all of them; and they will no longer be two nations, and no longer be divided into two kingdoms. . . . And they will be My people, and I will be their God. And My servant David will be king over them. . . . And I will make a covenant of peace with them; it will be an everlasting covenant with them" (Ezek. 37:21–24, 26).[19]

Israel was looking forward to the day when the Messiah would appear and fulfill that promise. Jesus probably chose twelve disciples in part to show the significance of his ministry and identity as the promised Messiah. They were to represent the twelve tribes that would one day be restored. In fact, Jesus promised them a place in his messianic kingdom: "Just as My Father has granted Me a kingdom, I grant you that you may eat and drink at My table in My kingdom, and you will sit on thrones judging the twelve tribes of Israel" (Luke 22:29–30).

The twelve were from a variety of backgrounds: some were fishermen, two were zealots (fanatical Jewish nationalists), and one was working for the Romans as a tax collector. Jesus had more than a hundred followers, but he created this inner circle with three characteristics:

1. There were twelve.
2. They were all Jewish.
3. They were all men.

Why were they all Jewish men? Jesus's primary ministry was to the Jews. His disciples were chosen to represent the twelve tribes that would someday reinhabit Israel when Jesus returned. So there had to be twelve, and the twelve had to be Jewish. But why were they all men?

---

19. Also, in Isa. 49:6 God said of the Messiah: "It is too small a thing that You should be My Servant to raise up the tribes of Jacob and to restore the protected ones of Israel; I will also make You a light of the nations so that My salvation may reach to the end of the earth."

In light of the ways Jesus treated women as well as God's ultimate plan for a church composed of both Jews and Gentiles, it may seem a bit surprising. But Jesus had a future in mind for those particular men. They were to become apostles. The Greek word, *apostolos*, means *messenger* or *delegate*. The twelve were going to be empowered to lay the foundation of the church.

Jesus had come for the Jew first, then also for the Gentile. The apostles were to be advocates of the gospel message to the Jewish leaders of their time. It was highly unlikely those leaders would give any credence to either a woman or a Gentile attempting to convince them of the truth. So being male would be important to what lay ahead for the twelve. It would help them fulfill God's intended purpose.

Does that mean that Jesus would then require all of the leaders in his church to be male? It might be true, but only if all *three* requirements were adhered to. While the church did begin in Jerusalem, it quickly spread to those outside that people group. In Acts 1:8, we see that Jesus charged his disciples to function as firsthand witnesses to what they had seen and experienced with him to the rest of the world (Judea, Samaria, and then the remotest part of the earth). Gentile and Jew were no longer divided: all were given the opportunity to believe. The vast majority of the church would be Gentile. Being Jewish is not a consideration in church leadership around the world today.

So if the Jewish "requirement" would not remain as a standard for church leaders, why would the male gender requirement remain? If you insist on one, it wouldn't make sense to ignore the other.

Not once did Jesus expect anything different from his female followers than he did of his male disciples. Never did he express limitations on what they could become. All through the Gospels, he treated them as equal to men. He encouraged them to be theologians, and treated women "with a degree of dignity, intelligence, camaraderie, and genuine brotherly love that was uncommon in those times."[20]

---

20. Marg Mowczko, "The Twelve Apostles Were All Male," *Marg Mowczko* (blog), May 2, 2012, https://margmowczko.com/the-twelve-apostles-were-all-male/. See also Ben Witherington III, professor of Biblical Interpretation at Asbury Theological Seminary, in an interview with Simon Smart from the Centre

Both the cultural attitudes toward women and how Jesus treated them are important contexts to our understanding of the New Testament. In the next chapter (on Acts), we will see that women were indeed included in every way as the church exploded into life.

Good News for Today

While we discuss the position of women in God's plan, it's important not to lose sight of the Main Thing. Our main focus needs to be on the Lord Jesus Christ. He is the example for all who follow him. God is transforming all believers, conforming them to his image. However we land on the women's issue, it must not pull us off the narrow road he wants us to travel.

Jesus never wavered from obeying the will of the Father. In his first advent, he left his glory, his equality with God, behind. He chose a life of submission and love, serving in humility, reaching out to the oppressed and insignificant (see Phil. 2:5–8). He did not demand glory or honor from his followers, only trust. The Good Shepherd tended carefully to his sheep. Not one was forgotten. Every single one was important to him.

Unfortunately, when our passions are inflamed, and we go into battle for what we believe is right, people in our path can get trampled. The cause easily becomes so much more important than loving our neighbor—one of the two greatest commandments, according to Jesus.

His works of power and authority, like calming the sea or turning a few loaves of bread and fish into enough to feed thousands, were not to extract an exalted place of honor from those who followed. They were signs, proof that his teachings were valid and from God. Jesus was all about the kingdom of God.

While we were in our twenties, my husband and I were part of a small church that held a Communion service first thing on Sunday mornings. It was informal in that there was no other agenda but to

---

for Public Christianity in Australia at https://vimeo.com/14172103, accessed January 7, 2022.

focus on Jesus—his life, his death, his resurrection—as the Spirit led men to speak. One day someone wrote a note to the elders requesting them to allow women to also verbally share at that weekly meeting. Wanting to get this right, the elders agreed to take time to study together all of the passages thought to limit women.

Over a year later, as the elders neared the end of their study, an angry group of church members arrived without warning at the elders' meeting. They were vehemently opposed to any change in our Communion service. It was a terrible scene. My husband (an elder) arrived home very late that night, deeply disturbed. "I feel like we just got hit by a tornado," he told me.

The following Sunday morning at coffee break, it became very clear who was on the side of change and who was not. One group talked together on one side of the room, the other across from them. Distrust had destroyed our former unity and fellowship. It was a different church than it had been a week ago.

We went on like that for several months, until the group wanting change was led to begin a new work. (The church that grew out of that is now over eight hundred strong.) Those who were left behind were steeped in bitterness. Sundays became an ordeal for Steve and me, as we chose to stay behind in hopes that God would use us to begin the healing we knew he wanted to do.

One December evening before that split, I stood outside the church talking with a friend. Her husband was not a believer, but he had been showing interest, coming to church with her for several months. She told me with tears in her eyes, "He's not going to be coming anymore. He said that the way people are treating each other has disgusted him. He thinks that people in this church are no different than anyone else. He now thinks Jesus is making zero difference in their lives."

As sad as this story is, it becomes even sadder in light of the fact that our church was not alone. I've heard too many stories about power struggles in churches. As followers of Jesus, we have somehow lost our priority for the Main Thing. The idea of the first being last and the last being first has been abandoned. Like the disciples wanting to be the greatest in the kingdom, we strive for importance or honor and can become rather nasty when others fail to approve of our cause. Power and influence trump humility and service. We ignore the perspective Jesus urged. We have failed to align ourselves with the Cornerstone.

When secondary doctrines become more important than kingdom values, when Christ is no longer at the center of our ideas and agendas, we are in a dangerous place. Always, always, Christ must be preeminent. It is all too easy to have our hearts pulled away from him in pursuit of a cause. Whatever is not centered on Christ will become warped. He is the pure and holy standard that will stand up to anything that has taken us off track. We must compare how we act on any issue with him: he whose humility, meekness, and love tempered every action and word.

Yes, there is a great divide on the issue of a woman's biblical role in the church and home. I've heard scandalous talk from all sides. People feel free to attack someone's ministry or character in order to win the argument and show everyone they are right. It's victory at all cost.

But that's what the world does.

How we handle the situation is telling; Paul said, "Be angry, and yet do not sin . . . and do not give the devil an opportunity" (Eph. 4:26–27). How many effective ministries have been damaged because of sinful behavior from fellow believers? I can tell you that, unfortunately, that little church of ours no longer exists. One by one, people left the bitter environment in search of peace.

As the body of Christ, we should know there is a better way. We can have unity despite differences. We can discuss these issues with love and respect, because that's how Jesus interacted with sinners. And if we can't, maybe it's time to examine our motives. When an issue causes us to treat others like scum or to abandon the rest of the church in the name of our cause, it's not from God. It has become about winning. Maybe it's time to reevaluate.

Chapter 5

What Kind of Ministry Roles Did Women Fill in the Early Church?

Then they returned to Jerusalem from the mountain called Olivet, which is near Jerusalem, a Sabbath day's journey away. When they had entered the city, they went up to the upstairs room where they were staying, that is, Peter, John, James, and Andrew, Philip and Thomas, Bartholomew and Matthew, James the son of Alphaeus, Simon the Zealot, and Judas the son of James. All these were continually devoting themselves with one mind to prayer, along with the women, and Mary the mother of Jesus, and with His brothers.

—Acts 1:12–14

> "And it shall be in the last days," God says,
> "That I will pour out My Spirit on all mankind;
> And your sons and your daughters will prophesy,
> And your young men will see visions,
> And your old men will have dreams;
> And even on My male and female servants
> I will pour out My Spirit in those days,
> And they will prophesy."

—Acts 2:17–18

Now a Jew named Apollos, an Alexandrian by birth, an eloquent man, came to Ephesus; and he was proficient in the Scriptures. This man had been instructed in the way of the Lord; and being fervent in spirit, he was accurately speaking and teaching things about Jesus, being acquainted only with the baptism of John; and he began speaking boldly in the synagogue. But when Priscilla and Aquila heard him, they took him aside and explained the way of God more accurately to him.

—Acts 18:24–26

I commend to you our sister Phoebe, a deacon of the church in Cenchreae. I ask you to receive her in the Lord in a way worthy of his people and to give her any help she may need from you, for she has been the benefactor of many people, including me.

Greet Priscilla and Aquila, my co-workers in Christ Jesus. They risked their lives for me. Not only I but all the churches of the Gentiles are grateful to them.

Greet also the church that meets at their house. . . .

Greet Mary, who worked very hard for you.

Greet Andronicus and Junia, my fellow Jews who have been in prison with me. They are outstanding among the apostles, and they were in Christ before I was.

—Romans 16:1–7 (NIV)

Focus on the Book of Acts

As I approached the last semester of seminary, I registered for my final classes, which included one called "Sermon Preparation." I was already doing a fair amount of speaking for women's groups and had looked forward to this class since I began seminary.

Soon after, my advisor gave me unexpected bad news. "You can't take Sermon Preparation," he told me apologetically, "because that class is only open to men." Right away, I knew why—the thought of a woman preaching from the pulpit was unacceptable for many of the professors and patrons of the school.

But I wasn't going down without a fight. "Seriously," I pleaded, "this class is one of the reasons I came to seminary! God has already given me an active speaking ministry for women. I need this class to help me develop my skills! Will you go to bat for me?"

God bless my advisor; he did go back and plead my case. A few weeks later, he gave me good news: the board had reconsidered. They would allow me to take the course. But they were changing its name. The class would now be called "*Message* Preparation."

As silly as that false dichotomy seemed to me, I gratefully enrolled. That next semester, the class was as valuable as I knew it would be.

At the time, the possibility of speaking from a Sunday morning pulpit wasn't even on my radar. But after that little bump in the road, I did wonder: were women limited in this way in the early church? Like Deborah in the Old Testament, women in Acts like Priscilla and Lydia sure seemed to function as leaders and teachers alongside men. It was time to give Acts and the women specifically named in the epistles a closer look.

The book of Acts opens as Jesus prepared to ascend back to heaven. He gathered his disciples one final time and gave them their marching orders. He told them not to leave Jerusalem just yet, but to wait for the promised Holy Spirit. "You will receive power when the Holy Spirit has come upon you; and you shall be My witnesses both in Jerusalem, and in all Judea, and Samaria, and as far as the remotest part of the earth" (Acts 1:8).

Luke tells us, "All these were continually devoting themselves with one mind to prayer, along with the women, and Mary the mother of Jesus, and with His brothers" (Acts 1:14). The group of believers that waited in Jerusalem at that time numbered around one hundred twenty (see Acts 1:15).

In our previous chapter, we saw how Jesus clearly valued and included women in his teaching and healing ministry. So it shouldn't surprise us to see their continued commitment in the days following his resurrection. The women were in it for life. Men and women waited as one unified body, prayerfully preparing to get to work.

How Does Luke Portray Women in the Book of Acts?

Luke, a physician by trade, wrote two volumes to a man named Theophilus: one a biography of Jesus Christ, the other a record of the church of Jesus Christ. When studying these books, the reader cannot help but notice how mindful and respectful Luke is toward women. This is striking considering the attitudes of his time, when patriarchy was commonplace and dictated the conventions of society.

Luke records a conversation on resurrection day between Jesus and two disciples on the road to Emmaus. Their remark to Jesus testifies as to women's inclusion: "But also some women *among us* left us bewildered" (Luke 24:22, emphasis mine).

Now, within fourteen verses from the beginning of Acts, we are told that women prayed in the upper room with the men as they jointly waited for God. Women remained present when Peter led the discussion on who would replace the now-deceased Judas Iscariot as the twelfth disciple. And, as the events of Acts 2 unfolded a few days later, women received the Holy Spirit and participated in the first major effort to bring the gospel to unbelievers.[1]

It was fifty days after the resurrection, the day of Pentecost, which celebrated the first harvest of the growing season.[2] This was an important observance and required Jews to celebrate in Jerusalem. During the festivities, the town's normal number of 30,000 residents temporarily swelled to a population of 80,000.[3] The streets were crowded with Jewish pilgrims from every country in the known world.

When the Holy Spirit suddenly arrived in the house where the group waited, it was dramatic, to say the least. A sound like a strong, rushing wind filled the room; what looked like tongues of fire came to rest on each person present. They were filled with the Holy Spirit and began to speak in foreign languages previously unknown to them. They spilled out into the streets and began to proclaim the good news that the Messiah had come, providing peace with God through his death and resurrection.

As the pilgrims from other lands heard the message in their native tongues, they were floored. How in the world could people from Galilee be so adept at their language?

Peter stood before the questioning crowd. He declared the words of the prophet Joel were being fulfilled, when the Lord said, "And it shall be in the last days . . . that I will pour out My Spirit on all mankind; and *your sons and your daughters* will prophesy, and your young men will see visions, and your old men will have dreams; and even on

---

1. Peter's citing of Joel 2:28–32 seems to reference the women's presence and involvement: "And your sons and your daughters will prophesy . . . even on the male and female servants I will pour out My Spirit in those days" (vv. 28–29). Peter indicates that what the crowd is seeing is a fulfillment of that prophecy. So it stands to reason women were involved, since they are twice specifically named.
2. Barley was the first, the culmination of the harvest season would be celebrated at Rosh Hashanah. See also Michelle Lee-Barnewall, *Neither Complementarian nor Egalitarian: A Kingdom Corrective to the Evangelical Gender Debate* (Grand Rapids: Baker Academic, 2016), 99.
3. Estimates of Jerusalem's population from ancient sources in the first century vary widely.

My *male and female* servants I will pour out My Spirit in those days, and they will prophesy" (Acts 2:17–18, emphasis mine).

At the very commencement of the church, men and women were indwelled by the Spirit and presumably served side by side.[4] Joel gave this prophecy in 835 BC, about 860 years before it was fulfilled that day at Pentecost. It had always been God's intention for women to serve right along with the men (reversing the patriarchy resulting from the consequences for the first sin).[5] Peter and the other apostles considered those events a fulfillment of Joel's prophecy (as they obviously were); for them, the specific inclusion of women was a sign it was the beginning of a new age.[6]

As time went on and the gospel spread, we see women mentioned specifically by name in Acts, revealed as active participants in the quickly developing church. These are the women listed:

- Tabitha (or Greek: Dorcas, Acts 9:36–42). Tabitha was known for her handiwork as a seamstress and her abundant good deeds of kindness and charity. She died suddenly from an illness. Upon notice of her death, Peter arrived and raised her from the dead. The miracle became known far and wide, and many believed in the Lord because of it.
- Mary, Mother of John Mark (Acts 12:12). It was at Mary's home that many disciples gathered to pray for Peter's release from Herod's prison. (James had already been put to death

---

4. Was it only the twelve who received the Holy Spirit? Luke tells us in Acts 2:41 that three thousand that day received the message and believed. But he also mentioned that each one was "bewildered, because each one of them was hearing them speak in his own language" (v. 6). How did three thousand people hear just twelve men? It is much more likely that the 120 scattered outdoors in order to spread out through Jerusalem. Eventually they made their way to the temple. The grounds of the temple were the only place within the city (with its restrictive, narrow streets) large enough for those thousands to hear Peter preach.
5. See comments on God's proclamation on Eve on pages 40–42 in chapter 2.
6. John Temple Bristow, *What Paul Really Said about Women: An Apostle's Liberating Views on Equality in Marriage, Leadership, and Love* (San Francisco: HarperCollins, 1991), 58.

by order of Herod.) Peter's first idea for a safe place to go after the angel rescued him was Mary's house. When he arrived, the believers there rejoiced to see him alive and free. Many scholars theorize that Mary's upper room was the same room where Jesus celebrated his Last Supper,[7] which would have meant Mary was a disciple before Jesus's death and resurrection.

- Lydia (Acts 16:14–15, 40). During his second missionary trip, Paul met this successful businesswoman outside the city of Philippi. A Gentile God-seeker[8] originally from Thyatira, Lydia was a successful businesswoman and had a large home with servants (no husband is mentioned). Paul, Silas, Timothy, and Luke found her and other women by the river, worshiping on the Sabbath (there were not enough Jewish men to warrant a synagogue in Philippi). They sat down and shared the gospel with them. Lydia believed, and she and her household were immediately baptized. The other new believers began meeting in her home.

- Leading Women in Thessalonica (Acts 17:4). Persuaded by Paul's preaching that Jesus was the Christ (the promised Messiah) and the Son of God, these women joined ranks with other believers identifying with Paul and Silas's message (equally recognized by Luke as an early part of the body of Christ).

---

7. Mary's son John Mark adds a unique detail to the night of Jesus's arrest in his Gospel account: a young man was seized by the temple guards wearing nothing but a linen sheet draped around him in the Garden of Gethsemane. He made his escape by pulling free of the sheet and running away naked (Mark 14:51–52). Some theorize that earlier, John Mark had been asleep in his mother's home (after watching the Passover meal) and was awakened by the high priest's associates seeking to arrest Jesus. (When Judas left to report Jesus's whereabouts to them, Jesus was still in the upper room. So Judas would have taken the guards there first.) It is possible John Mark heard them, and in panic, wrapped up in the nearest covering and dashed off to the garden to warn Jesus of their imminent approach. There in the garden the guards seized him, and he made his awkward escape.

8. God-seeker or worshiper of God: Gentiles who are trained in but not yet converted to Judaism.

- Damaris (Acts 17:34). While in Athens, Paul preached his famous sermon from Mars Hill. Some Athenians believed: Luke specifically mentions a man named Dionysius the Areopagite and a woman named Damaris, along with unnamed others.
- Priscilla (Acts 18:2, 18, 26). Priscilla and her husband Aquila met Paul while he was in Corinth during his second missionary journey. They were refugees from Rome, where the emperor Claudius had recently ordered all Jews to leave. Paul ended up staying with them for a year and a half in Corinth and partnering with them in the business of tent making. When Paul finally moved on, Priscilla and Aquila traveled with him, and Paul left them in Ephesus to continue the work in Galatia. Luke also adds that Priscilla and Aquila worked with a talented, enthusiastic Alexandrian preacher named Apollos. His only exposure to Jesus had been through John the Baptist's ministry, so the couple pulled him aside to teach him everything about Jesus. Thanks to their instruction, Apollos went on to be a powerful orator, expertly demonstrating through Old Testament Scriptures that Jesus was the Messiah.
- Philip's Four Daughters (Acts 21:9). Philip was one of the seven named deacons in Jerusalem tasked to oversee the distribution of food to those in need (see Acts 6:1–6). Paul stopped at Philip's house on his way to Jerusalem before his arrest. Luke tells us Philip had four virgin daughters who were prophets and whose gifts would have involved preaching God's words to the church (see Acts 21:8–9).

What Was Paul's General Attitude Toward Women?

Before the crucifixion, Jesus prayed for unity in the church: "That they may all be one; just as You, Father, are in Me and I in You . . . so that the world may believe that You sent Me" (John 17:21). The effectiveness of the church in revealing Jesus would be dependent on how well believers loved and cared for each other (especially in light of their differences).

Paul aligned himself with Jesus's concern. Several of his epistles were written to specifically address issues that divided. The church at Corinth allowed social status to determine importance within the fellowship. Groups in both Rome and Ephesus were one-upping each other as to who was more deserving: Jews, who had claim to being the chosen race, or Gentiles, who felt the Jews had all the information they needed to know about God, yet kept their hearts from him.

Paul worked to destroy any barriers to unity: "For you are all sons of God through faith in Christ Jesus. For all of you who were baptized into Christ have clothed yourselves with Christ. There is neither Jew nor Greek, there is neither slave nor free man, there is neither male nor female, for you are all one in Christ Jesus" (Gal. 3:26–28 NASB1995). With that single sentence, Paul eliminated demarcations between any factions whose natural inclination toward each other was hostility and suspicion.[9]

Paul considered every believer to be a new creation, baptized into Christ. All believers have been given the ministry of reconciliation (bringing people to God) and are to function as ambassadors for Christ (see 2 Cor. 5:17–21). He also taught, as Peter did, of all believers "being built up as a spiritual house for a holy priesthood, to offer spiritual sacrifices acceptable to God through Jesus Christ" (1 Peter 2:5). Paul wrote to the Ephesians: "You are fellow citizens with the saints, and are of God's household . . . growing into a holy temple in the Lord, in whom you also are being built together into a dwelling of God in the Spirit" (Eph. 2:19, 21–22). In light of his convictions, we can rest assured that Paul valued and respected women as equal members in the body of Christ.

Did Paul Identify Women Leaders in His Letters?

In Greco-Roman culture, it was not proper to extend public recognition to women. But Paul defied convention and commended women

---

9. Lee-Barnewall, *Neither Complementarian*, 101.

for their service in the same way he commended men.[10] His value for every worker (regardless of gender) is especially apparent in the greetings and acknowledgments at the close of his letters. He commends women with the very same language he uses for men in describing their contribution to the kingdom.

When we see a name in Paul's letters, it very likely means that they were already known for laudable Christian service and ministry; their names would be familiar in every church that received Paul's writings. They may not all be specifically identified as leaders, but the number of women Paul mentions in Romans 16 accounts for about one-third of the total mentions in that letter.[11]

- Phoebe (Romans 16:1–2 NIV). Paul commends Phoebe, who had carried his letter to the Romans, and asks that they receive her in "a manner worthy of the saints." He describes her as a "deacon of the church which is at Cenchrea." The Greek word *diakonos* can mean servant or minister, and is the same word he uses for the church office of deacon in 1 Timothy 3 and Philippians 1.[12]

  Paul also calls Phoebe a *prostatis*, which meant a patron or benefactor.[13] This feminine noun occurs only once in the New

---

10. Cynthia Long Westfall, *Paul and Gender: Reclaiming the Apostle's Vision for Men and Women in Christ* (Grand Rapids: Baker Academic, 2016), 223.

11. There are twenty-six names, seven of them women's.

12. Lynn Cohick also writes: "About ten years into the second century AD, Pliny the Younger, governor of Bithynia, wrote to Emperor Trajan that he had arrested two female deaconesses or *ministrae*, beaten them, and questioned them about their cult, Christianity . . . the title was also used in an inscription noting freedwomen who donated their own money to build a temple to the *Bona Dea* . . . they were questioned as though they could give an accurate testimony of this prohibited group. . . . From another second century figure, Celsus's infamous condemnation has sounded throughout centuries—Christianity is a religion of women and slaves." Lynne Cohick, *Women in the World of the Earliest Christians: Illuminating Ways of Life* (Grand Rapids: Baker Academic, 2009), 195.

13. Walter Baur, *A Greek-English Lexicon of the New Testament and Other Early Christian Literature*, 3rd ed., ed. Frederick William Danker, W. F. Arndt, and F. W. Gingrich (Chicago: University of Chicago Press, 2000), 885 (hereafter

Testament. However, when the masculine form of *prostatis* is used, it connotes authority or rule over another.[14] Its verb form, *proistēmi*, means "to exercise a position of leadership, rule, direct, be the head of."[15]

Some scholars propose that one who delivered a letter also read it to its recipients, giving its largely illiterate "hearers . . . the correct tone and emphasis as if from Paul himself."[16] So, Phoebe could have been tasked with explaining the letter to the church after it was read. This would have required quite a bit of theological understanding.[17]

- Priscilla (Romans 16:3–5). Now back in Rome, Priscilla and her husband Aquila are greeted by Paul as his "fellow workers" who, for the sake of Paul's life, "risked their own necks." He adds to his own thanks the gratitude of "all the churches of the Gentiles" for their faithful ministry. He greets those who meet at their house church there in Rome as well. Before returning there, Priscilla and Aquila hosted another house church while in Asia (see 1 Cor. 16:19). In the Greco-Roman world, when authors listed people in writing, they frequently did so in order of importance. It is worth noting that when the couple's names are found in Scripture, Priscilla (sometimes called

---

cited as BDAG). According to Thayer, the first meaning of *prostatis* is "a woman set over others." Joseph Thayer, ed., *A Greek Lexicon of the New Testament* (New York: American Book Co., 1886), 549. The masculine form of this word was used by Justin Martyr for a person who presided at Communion, and by Paul in Rom. 12:8 (translated in the NASB1995 as "he who leads"). The word almost always refers to an officially recognized position of authority. Alice Mathews, *Gender Roles and the People of God: Rethinking What We Were Taught about Men and Women in the Church* (Grand Rapids: Zondervan, 2017), 86.

14. Lucy Peppiatt, *Unveiling Paul's Women: Making Sense of 1 Corinthians 11:2–16* (Eugene, OR: Cascade Books, 2018), 126.

15. BDAG, *proistēmi*, 871.

16. Lucy Peppiatt, *Rediscovering Scripture's Vision for Women: Fresh Perspectives on Disputed Texts* (Downers Grove, IL: InterVarsity Press, 2019), 125. According to William Sheill, this was the job of the lector in Greco-Roman times. William Sheill, *Reading Acts: The Lector and the Early Christian Audience* (Leiden: Brill, 2004).

17. Peppiatt, *Rediscovering*, 125.

Prisca) is named first in four out of six occurrences. This could well mean that she was the more prominent of the two.

- Junia (Romans 16:7 NIV). Paul greets two people, named Andronicus and Junia, who are his "kinfolk and my fellow prisoners." (Several centuries ago, doubt was cast on the female gender of Junia, but scholars today are pretty much in agreement that Junia was a woman.) Paul calls her and Andronicus "outstanding among the apostles, and they were in Christ before I was."

When Peter explained the necessary qualifications of a replacement apostle in Acts 1, he said it would have to be someone who had been with them during Jesus's ministry on earth (see Acts 1:21–22). Why? They were to be witnesses; so only a firsthand experience with Jesus would do; a second-hand testimony could have been considered mere hearsay. Since Junia was a disciple in the earliest days, it is likely she had encountered Jesus while he ministered on earth (see Rom. 16:7).

Did the words "among the apostles" mean Paul considered Junia an apostle? No one had trouble with the idea that Junia was an apostle until it was proved by scholars that Junia was a woman's name.[18] Those who objected to the possibility that a woman could be an apostle suddenly reinterpreted "outstanding among the apostles" to mean that the apostles appreciated their contribution, not that they were apostles themselves. Peppiatt comments: "It should be noted that while translators believed Junia to be a man, there was no such ambiguity."[19] The literal translation of Paul's phrasing is "who are notable among the apostles."[20]

One of the early church fathers, John Chrysostom, wrote

---

18. The spelling of the Greek name in manuscripts was *Junian*, which is the accusative form of the feminine form of Junia.
19. Peppiatt, *Rediscovering*, 122.
20. Bristow, *What Paul Really Said*, 57.

of Junia: "Oh how great is the devotion of this woman, that she should be even counted worthy of the appellation of apostle!"[21]

- Mary (Romans 16:6). Paul greets Mary and reminds the Romans that she has "worked hard for you."
- Tryphaena and Tryphosa (Romans 16:12). Paul identifies these two women as "workers in the Lord." (He uses the designation of "worker" in verse 21 for Timothy and himself.)

Throughout Romans 16, Paul gives a personal greeting to a large number of people. Out of the twenty-six people he names, seven of them are women, with two additional unnamed women referenced as well. Women and men are mixed together, but all are workers whom he commends. There is no differentiation between genders in how they are greeted and valued in this passage. Other women mentioned in Romans 16: Persis, Rufus's mother, and Julia.

In some of his other epistles, Paul again mentions several outstanding women. He asks that *Euodia* and *Syntyche* (Phil. 4:2–3) live in harmony in the Lord, and comments that these women "shared my struggle in the cause of the gospel, together with Clement as well as the rest of my fellow workers, whose names are in the book of life." He was informed by "*Chloe's* people" of quarrels among the Corinthians (1 Cor. 1:11). *Nympha* had a church meeting in her house (Col. 4:15), which was a notable responsibility that would have included leadership within the group.[22]

There are others Paul named in a special greeting, but he does not mention anything more than their names. Even so, what Paul did write about the women actively ministering in the first century should give us confidence that God's intent for the church is for us to eliminate the idea of gender boundaries today.

21. Bristow, *What Paul Really Said*, 57.
22. Cynthia Long Westfall, *Paul and Gender* (Grand Rapids: Baker Academic, 2016), 232.

Good News for Today

Years ago, my friend Julie, who is fluent in Spanish, began a ministry teaching English and US history and government to immigrants seeking citizenship. Some of her students began to attend her church and asked for the sermons to be interpreted for them. A new ministry was born. She and three others worked to interpret every Sunday from the church library on a rotating basis.

One Sunday morning, while Julie was busy translating, someone with a camera walked into the room, looked at her, then left. She didn't give it a second thought. But later that day, she got a call from one of the other translators.

"Julie, I thought you should know that Mike, Bob, and I were called to the church to pose for a picture," he said. "Apparently, leadership plans to run an article about our ministry in the church newsletter. We asked where you were, and they told us they didn't want you in the photo because you are a woman. We told them that you were the one who started the ministry with the immigrants—if it weren't for you, it wouldn't exist. We said if you weren't in the picture, then we weren't going to be in it either."

She later heard that the church staff decided to drop the article altogether.

Fortunately, Paul had no such reservations. He had worked for the cause of the gospel with a number of women in many different locations. He publicly expressed warm greetings to each of them, often including remarks that would garner respect for them among his recipients.

As we saw in Genesis 3, patriarchy was not designed by God. His design was that males and females would rule and subdue the earth together. Sin affected every part of his creation, including the relationship between males and females. Eve was told that rather than the oneness she had experienced before biting into that forbidden fruit, she would be ruled over by man.

But Jesus came to reverse the effects of sin. No longer would sin control the hearts of those who believed in him (Rom. 6:12–14). Paul knew that the Holy Spirit's indwelling would make us a *new creation* (see John 6:63; 2 Cor. 5:17). Men and women would once again, for the first time since the garden, be able to operate within God's original design.

In light of what we have seen in both the book of Acts and Paul's letters, I would say that Paul would have been appalled at Julie's church's refusal to acknowledge her part in the ministry. He valued women in the early church and continually worked toward erasing any kind of demarcation between all factions.

I'm happy to report that five years later, Julie was able to visit the area again and attended her former church that Sunday. She found out there was a Hispanic church now meeting in the building; so of course, she went. One of the translators who had worked with her was giving the announcements when she walked in. There were about one hundred people in attendance. Thrilled at what God had done, she settled in to enjoy the service. As she listened, she mused: nothing she had done in her time there had resulted in this kind of fruit. Had God waited to bless the effort until a man had been put in charge? Had she been disobedient in taking initiative as a woman?

At the end of the service, her translator friend stood to make a final announcement. "We have a very special visitor today. Most of you don't know Julie, but she is the one who started International Friends ministry, from which this church grew. Without her, this church would not exist."

The response from the audience rocked her. Almost every person in attendance came up and hugged her, expressing gratitude for her work on their behalf. Now, these years later, Julie understands that experience as an affirmation from God, who led her to serve in that ministry. Being a woman was not an impediment to God as he worked through her to build his church.

I have no doubt that Paul would agree with Julie. In fact, in our next chapter, as we study what he had to say about spiritual gifts, I'm pretty sure you will agree that gender does not impede God's work. God has called both men and women to lead. No longer does patriarchy dictate how we should operate, dividing the church with gender barriers. In our redemption through Jesus Christ, we are free to serve as one, as God designed his church to function.

Chapter 6

Are Men to Be Given Precedence in the Church?

Now I praise you because you remember me in everything and hold firmly to the traditions, just as I handed them down to you. But I want you to understand that Christ is the head of every man, and the man is the head of a woman, and God is the head of Christ. Every man who has something on his head while praying or prophesying disgraces his head. But every woman who has her head uncovered while praying or prophesying disgraces her head, for it is one and the same as the woman whose head is shaved. For if a woman does not cover her head, have her also cut her hair off; however, if it is disgraceful for a woman to have her hair cut off or her head shaved, have her cover her head. For a man should not have his head covered, since he is the image and glory of God; but the woman is the glory of man. For man does not originate from woman, but woman from man; for indeed man was not created for the woman's sake, but woman for the man's sake. Therefore the woman should have a symbol of authority on her head, because of the angels. However, in the Lord, neither is woman independent of man, nor is man independent of woman. For as the woman originated from the man, so also the man has his birth through the woman; and all things originate from God. Judge for yourselves: is it proper for a woman to pray to God with her head uncovered? Does even nature itself not teach you that if a man has long hair, it is a dishonor to him, but if a woman has long hair, it is a glory to her? For her hair is given to her as a covering. But if anyone is inclined to be contentious, we have no such practice, nor have the churches of God.

—1 Corinthians 11:2–16

Focus on 1 Corinthians 11:1–16

Years ago, I was asked to speak for pastors' wives and other female church leaders at a statewide denominational conference. The committee that organized the event went all out in planning the food, the program, and beautiful fall décor. It was the only event during the conference specifically for the women, and they were determined to make it a special time for all involved.

But you know what they say about best-laid plans. At the last minute, the night before, the conference leadership decided to add an early morning prayer session into the schedule. This pushed the entire day's events back one hour. They decided to make up for the lost hour by cutting the women's banquet time allotment in half.

When we arrived at the venue, the committee was scrambling to make the unexpected time restriction work. As the women came in, they were sent straight to the buffet line that had people stationed in several spots urging them to get their food quickly. Many were still waiting to fill their plates when my daughter was asked to start the worship portion of the program.

When I was introduced, the women hadn't even had a chance to exchange pleasantries, never mind finish eating. I wasn't sure anyone was listening as I began. It was a speaker's nightmare. But the worst moment came near the end of my message when the director of the conference came in and began to quietly chastise the banquet committee chair. Why wasn't it over yet? He was angry with her because of a problem of his own making.

I was in disbelief that he wasn't at least a little apologetic about ruining their big event. Instead, he reduced that chairwoman to tears. He didn't have the slightest interest in what was happening in that room. The women didn't matter at all. The only event catered to them was expendable in his mind.

From where did this attitude come? Why would someone feel justified in disregarding their women's needs to such a disgraceful extent? Why would it be assumed that men should have priority?

It's likely, had I been given the opportunity to question his mind-set, he would have quoted a verse that is often used to give men superiority over women in the church: "Christ is the head of every man, and *man is the head of a woman*, and God is the head of Christ" (1 Cor. 11:3, emphasis mine). Men are to lead, women to follow. Males have priority in matters of spiritual leadership. But is that what Paul meant when he penned this?

Of all the passages that specifically deal with women in the New Testament, I have found 1 Corinthians 11:1–16 to be the most challenging to understand. I'm not alone—most commentators are at odds with each other about Paul's intent. In light of the notorious difficulty these verses present, some people have actually concluded they were added into a later manuscript copy by a scribe!

This passage was written two thousand years ago. So we must, as much as is humanly possible, endeavor to view it through first-century Corinthian eyes. That will require learning as much as we can about Paul and his original readers. Before we can decide how this passage applies to us today, we have to know: what would these verses have meant to *them*? What was the principle Paul was trying to get across? Was he ordering men to be given precedence?[1]

A good place to start is to examine the passage through the lens of the literary tool Paul uses to address his subject. Paul was well-educated and used sophisticated writing in all of his letters. Peter

---

1. Ronald Pierce observes, "The argumentation as a whole is especially uncharacteristic of Paul, both in terms of his generally relaxed attitude to the presenting issue itself and of his arguing primarily on the basis of cultural shame rather than from the person and work of Christ." Ronald W. Pierce, "Women and Men in Christian Assembly" (lecture, Biola University, La Mirada, CA, April 2013), https://www.youtube.com/watch?v=lRW8dCfvaMg&list=PLYtr ZmQ7NN0CRA-gWcqZOvB5nmUuJ6FNe&index=10.

even wrote about how tricky it was for some to get the full meaning of Paul's writings: "Just as also our beloved brother Paul, according to the wisdom given him, wrote to you, as also in all his letters . . . in which there are some things that are hard to understand, which the untaught and unstable distort" (2 Peter 3:15–16). Identifying Paul's structure is key to a correct understanding.

How Was Paul Building His Argument?

Paul appears to be using a classic literary tool called a *chiasm,* or *chiastic structure.*[2] It is an arrangement that presents ideas in parallel statements, where one statement helps interpret the other. At the center of the parallel phrases is the most important or central idea. Paul was well-acquainted with chiastic structures, as much of the Old Testament is written in that form, and it was frequently used by rabbis in his day.

Here's a simple breakdown of 1 Corinthians 11:2–16:

A (vv. 2–3) Now I praise you because you . . . hold firmly to the traditions, just as I handed them down to you. But I want you to understand that Christ is the head of every man, and the man is the head of a woman, and God is the head of Christ.

> **B** (vv. 4–5) Every man who has something on his head while praying or prophesying disgraces his head. But every woman who has her head uncovered while praying or prophesying disgraces her head . . .

>> **C** (vv. 7–9) Man . . . is the image and glory of God; but the woman is the glory of man. For man does not originate from woman, but woman from man . . .

---

2. I owe this insight to Ronald Pierce, who skillfully teaches this in his lecture on "Women and Men in Christian Assembly," part of a class entitled "Theology of Gender" (Pierce, "Women and Men . . .").

D (v. 10): *center statement, stands alone.* **Therefore the woman should have a symbol of authority on her head, because of the angels**.

C₁ (vv. 11–12) However, in the Lord, neither is woman independent of man, nor is man independent of woman . . . and all things originate from God.

B₁ (vv. 13–15) Judge for yourselves: is it proper for a woman to pray to God with her head uncovered? Does even nature itself not teach you that if a man has long hair, it is a dishonor to him, but if a woman has long hair, it is a glory to her? For her hair is given to her as a covering.

A₁ (v. 16) We have no such practice, nor have the churches of God.

Let's take a look at each parallel pair, since one statement should help define the other. Both A and A₁ are about traditions, customs practiced in the church.

A Now I praise you because you . . . hold firmly to the traditions, just as I handed them down to you.

A₁ We have no such practice [custom, tradition], nor have the churches of God.

He begins and ends the chiasm with these statements. The custom under discussion is the practice (or tradition) of wearing head coverings in church.

The second pair of statements are as follows:

B Every man who has something on his head . . . disgraces his head. But every woman who has her head uncovered . . . disgraces her head.

B₁ Judge for yourselves: is it proper for a woman to pray to God with her head uncovered? Does even nature itself not teach you that if a man has long hair, it is a dishonor to him, but if a woman has long hair, it is a glory to her? For her hair is given to her as a covering.

These statements present a bit of a problem. In B, Paul says a woman without a head covering disgraces her head. But in B₁, Paul says that her hair is her head covering. So, if she is not bald, doesn't her hair count as a cover? This is confusing.

The third pair of statements gives the rationale behind B and B₁:

C Man . . . is the image and glory of God; but the woman is the glory of man. For man does not originate from woman, but woman from man . . .

C₁ However, in the Lord, neither is woman independent of man, nor is man independent of woman . . . all things originate from God.

With both statements, Paul is referring to creation order. In C, he cites woman originating from man. Yet in C₁, Paul disregards the order of creation and recognizes the fact that, in reality, all of us come from God. Doesn't one statement negate the other?

To make better sense of these challenges, we need to go back to the reasons Paul wrote the letter.

What Was the Situation in Corinth at the Time?

The city of Corinth was a vital link between Rome and its eastern provinces. Situated on an isthmus of land between two widely traveled bodies of water, it attracted traders from all over the world and teemed with commerce.[3] With such diverse influences, most pagan religions were represented in the general populace of Corinth.

3. David E. Garland, *1 Corinthians*, Baker Exegetical Commentary on the New

Rome had declared Corinth a Roman colony, and its proud citizens were zealous to attain public status, promote themselves, and secure power.[4] It was a culture of seeking honor.[5]

Paul planted the church in Corinth while on his second missionary journey around AD 50–51 (see Acts 18:1–22). He settled in long-term, continuing to preach the gospel and discipling his new converts for one and a half years. After departing, he continued his relationship with the church for years through correspondence.

The epistle we call 1 Corinthians was actually written sometime after a previous letter of Paul's (see 1 Cor. 5:9). The first letter has since been lost. He'd received their response to that first correspondence, and he'd also heard about their division issues from members of Chloe's household (1 Cor. 1:11). Now, with his second letter to them (that we now call 1 Corinthians), Paul follows up on the issues they'd raised.[6]

While we don't have a copy of the Corinthian believers' letter to him, we can surmise what was happening in Corinth by reading Paul's side of the correspondence.

- *Sexual immorality.* Corinth was a known center for pagan worship rites; prostitution in the temples of Aphrodite and other local gods set the tone for depravity within the city. From what Paul writes, it is apparent the Corinthians had not separated themselves from that activity: "It is actually reported that there is sexual immorality among you" (1 Cor. 5:1). "Flee sexual immorality. . . . Or do you not know that your body is a temple of the Holy Spirit within you, whom you have from God, and that you are not your own?" (1 Cor. 6:18–19).

- *Division in the body.* Surrounded by a culture of self-promotion, it is not surprising that the Corinthian church was marked

---

Testament (Baker Academic, Grand Rapids: 2003), 4.

4. Garland, *1 Corinthians*, 4.

5. Garland, *1 Corinthians*, 5.

6. Paul uses the Greek *peri de*, or "now concerning," in 1 Cor. 7:25; 8:1; 12:1; 16:1, 12.

with division and strife. Paul wrote, "Now I urge you, brothers and sisters, by the name of our Lord Jesus Christ, that you all agree and that there be no divisions among you, but that you be made complete in the same mind and in the same judgment. For I have been informed concerning you . . . that there are quarrels among you" (1 Cor. 1:10–11).

- *Split loyalties.* One dispute was over their choice of allegiance. Each group claimed whatever teacher they followed gave them one-upmanship in their spiritual status. Paul admonished: "I planted, Apollos watered, but God was causing the growth. So then neither the one who plants nor the one who waters is anything, but God who causes the growth" (1 Cor. 3:6–7). They were barking up the wrong tree. "But God has chosen the foolish things of the world to shame the wise, and God has chosen the weak things of the world to shame the things which are strong . . . so that *no human may boast before God*" (1 Cor. 1:27, 29, emphasis mine).

- *Self-promotion.* In true Corinthian form, church members were vying for the top tier on the spiritual ladder, which was opposite to the message of the gospel. At the foot of the cross, they were all on equal ground. All were completely dependent on God's mercy and grace. There was no hierarchy or self-importance there. God was the one at work in them, setting them apart for his kingdom. All credit for that work belonged to God alone.

  Certain pompous individuals had not gotten that message. They were encouraging social barriers and treating people according to their social status rather than as brothers and sisters in Christ. Paul wrote: "When you come together as a church, I hear that divisions exist . . . factions among you, so that those who are approved may become evident among you. . . . Do you despise the church of God and shame those who have nothing?" (1 Cor. 11:18–19, 22).

- *Communion issues.* Division in the body was most apparent when they gathered for the Lord's Supper. Those who had more discretionary time were meeting to eat together before the more menial workers were able to get there. This resulted in a clear and deliberate division of the classes. The church was exalting certain individuals at the expense of the community.[7] Again, such an attitude was an affront to the gospel that had saved them.

- *Personal squabbles.* Paul also criticized the way they were handling disputes: "Brother goes to law with brother, and that before unbelievers? Actually, then, it is already a defeat for you, that you have lawsuits with one another. Why not rather suffer the wrong?" (1 Cor. 6:6–7). Members were involving secular courts to settle their issues. They were not functioning as a body, but acting as individuals determined to win at any cost.

Apparently, the church was more a reflection of the secular society around them than an appropriate representation of the kingdom of God. Gordon Fee observes: "The problem was not that the church was in Corinth, but that too much of Corinth was in the church."[8] The Corinthians needed serious guidance on how to relate to each other.

What Is the Context of the Passage in Question?

We will need to consider the context of the rest of Paul's letter to understand what he wrote here in chapter 11. Why was Paul writing to the Corinthians in the first place? What specific issues was he addressing?

There were no chapter and verse divisions in the text until centuries later.[9] The original letter was one unified document, with no isolating

---

7. Garland, *1 Corinthians*, 13.
8. Gordon D. Fee, *The First Epistle to the Corinthians*, The New International Commentary on the New Testament (Grand Rapids: Eerdmans, 1987), 4.
9. In the fifth century, the Bible translator Jerome divided Scripture into short

sections or subtitles. Whatever meaning we eventually ascertain from this section, it has its place in the whole.

Chapter 11 is a part of a larger argument Paul has been working on since chapter 7. He is addressing the false dichotomy the Corinthians have advocated between

- husbands and wives (7:1–16)
- the circumcised and the uncircumcised (7:17–20)
- slaves and free men (7:21–24)
- single and married persons (7:24–40)
- those who ate food sacrificed to idols and those who did not (8:1–13)
- the privileged and the underprivileged (11:19–34)

Lines had been drawn in the sand every which way in Corinth. The priority of their hearts did not match the kingdom that Jesus preached. "If you greet only your brothers, what more are you doing than others? Do not even the Gentiles do the same?" (Matt. 5:47 NASB1995). Paul was calling them to treat each other, even in light of differences or conflict, as the brothers and sisters in Christ that they were. Just as Jesus had.

Following our passage, in chapter 12, Paul urges them to start thinking like a body, where every member is important and needed. They were all linked together as parts of a whole. Then in chapter 13, Paul describes love in practical, simple terms, showing them God's way of relating. In chapter 14, he urges oneness in the body in how they used and valued their spiritual gifts.

So it seems that we should understand 1 Corinthians 11:1–16 as one more entry to a list of dangerous factions that were tearing the church apart: inequality between men and women.

---

passages. The actual chapter division didn't happen until many years later: Stephen Langton divided the Bible into chapters in AD 1227. Our modern verse division was the work of Robert Stephanus, who published the Latin Vulgate in 1551.

What Questions Had the Corinthians Written to Paul?

If you will remember, this letter is Paul's response to the Corinthians' previous letter. Their letter to Paul would have been carried by a messenger, who had traveled quite a distance to deliver it. So as Paul responds, he reminds them what they had asked about several months earlier. We do the same with emails, copying and pasting sentences into a new email and then responding to them.

He begins in chapter 7: "*Now concerning the things about which you wrote. . .*"[10] The issue between men and women (behind the dispute about head coverings) is one of the things about which they wrote.

As we saw earlier, the big challenge in chapter 11 is that verses 2–10 seem to stand in opposition to verses 11–16. A plausible interpretation is that Paul first restates what *they* had written with vv. 2–10,[11] then responds: "However, in the Lord . . ." and commences a refutation of their assumptions with verses 11–16.

He seems to quote what they wrote: "Christ is the head [Greek: *kephale*] of every man, and the man is the head of a woman, and God is the head of Christ" (v. 3).

This raises a concern. We can understand man being the head of a woman, and Christ being the head of man, but God being the *head* of Christ?[12] This is a strange statement to have been coming from

---

10. First Cor. 7:1, 25; 8:1; 12:1; 16:1 all begin with the phrase "Now concerning . . ." What follows appear to be responses to what they stated or asked in their previous letter to him. "Now concerning the things about which you wrote, it is good for a man not to touch a woman" (7:1). "Now concerning virgins, I have no command of the Lord" (7:25). "Now concerning food sacrificed to idols, we know . . . that an idol is nothing at all in the world, and that there is no God but one" (8:1, 8:4). "Now concerning spiritual gifts . . ." (12:1). "Now concerning the collection for the saints . . ." (16:1). All are references from the letter he had received (and he now responds to them).

11. Unfortunately, where he may be quoting back their words is not easily identifiable, because the original language (Koine Greek) does not contain punctuation, including quotation marks.

12. The Septuagint is a translation of the Hebrew Old Testament into Greek. Looking at its use of vocabulary can be very helpful in learning how the New Testament writers would have thought of certain words and why they used them. Translators used a different word that also translates as head, *arche*, when identifying someone in authority. Biblical scholar Philip Payne observes that in

Paul, in light of what the rest of Scripture has to say about the deity of Jesus. But we must view these three statements here as corresponding. What is true of one must be true of the other two.

So we must ask: how is God the *head* of Christ? The Bible is very clear that Jesus and God (and the Holy Spirit) are one in being, power, and significance. John begins his Gospel with "In the beginning was the Word, and the Word was with God, and the *Word was God*" (John 1:1, emphasis mine). Jesus said, "I and the Father are *one*" (John 10:30, emphasis mine).

In John 5, Jesus told Jewish leaders after they accused him of working on the Sabbath, "My Father is working until now, and I Myself am working." John then explains: "For this reason therefore the Jews were seeking all the more to kill Him, because He not only was breaking the Sabbath, but also was calling God His own Father, *making Himself equal with God*" (John 5:17–18, emphasis mine).

Jesus also claimed authority to judge the nations and to forgive sins (see Matt. 25:31–46; Mark 2:5–7). These things were known from Old Testament writings to be things only God could do (see 1 Sam. 2:6–10; Isa. 43:25). Jewish leaders understood this. It is why they charged and convicted him of blasphemy—they didn't believe his claims to be God (see Luke 5:21; Mark 2:7).

The names of God are applied to Jesus in the Old Testament. In an Isaiah passage foretelling the coming Messiah, he is called "Mighty God, *Eternal Father*, Prince of Peace" (Isa. 9:6, emphasis mine). Micah's prophecy about the Messiah included "But as for you, Bethlehem Ephrathah, too little to be among the clans of Judah, from you One will come forth for Me to be ruler in Israel. His times of

---

only 6 of 171 instances where head might convey leader or one in charge was *kephale* used. Philip B. Payne, *Man and Woman, One in Christ: An Exegetical and Theological Study of Paul's Letters* (Grand Rapids: Zondervan, 2009), 119. *Kephale* was used to describe the source of a river, a physical top of something (like a mountain) or a literal head on a person's body. In English, our go-to meaning of head would be "in charge." But in Paul's day, they frequently used head (Greek: *kephale*) to indicate a "source," like the head of a river sources the water that flows out of it.

coming forth are from long ago, *from the days of eternity*" (Micah 5:2, emphasis mine).

Paul says of Christ in another letter: "For in Him *all the fullness of Deity dwells* in bodily form. . . . He is the head over every ruler and authority" (Col. 2:9–10, emphasis mine). But how does this equality with God reconcile with the fact that Jesus lived in complete obedience to the Father while on earth?

Paul explains it in Philippians 2: "Have this attitude in yourselves which was also in Christ Jesus, who, as He *already existed in the form of God, did not consider equality with God something to be grasped, but emptied Himself* by taking the form of a bond-servant and being born in the likeness of men. And being found in appearance as a man, He *humbled Himself by becoming obedient* to the point of death: death on a cross" (vv. 5–8, emphasis mine).

Notice that before leaving heaven, Jesus existed with the Father as an equal. But in order to become a man, he needed to give up his authority and glory for the time he would spend on earth. This was a temporary thing, done in order to complete his all-important redemption mission of representing humankind on the cross. Yes, he did live under the authority of the Father during his time on earth ("He humbled Himself by *becoming* obedient"). As Jesus said, "I can do nothing on My own initiative. . . . I do not seek My own will, but the will of Him who sent Me" (John 5:30 NASB1995).

But once Jesus ascended back to heaven, the glory and authority that he'd previously left behind were restored. Paul continues, "For this reason also God highly exalted Him, and bestowed on Him the name which is above every name, so that at the name of Jesus every knee will bow, of those who are in heaven and on earth and under the earth, and that every tongue will confess that Jesus Christ is Lord, to the glory of God the Father" (Phil. 2:9–11).

God cannot be the authority over Christ if they are equal. Jesus *is* God.[13] Payne observes: "If there is no permanent hierarchy of author-

---

13. There is a modern doctrine some believe called "The Eternal Subordination of

ity between God and Christ, then [1 Corinthians] 11:3 is ill-suited to support such a hierarchy between man and woman."[14]

A second statement from 1 Corinthians 11:4–6 gets specific about head coverings:

> Every man who has something on his head while praying or prophesying disgraces his head. But every woman who has her head uncovered while praying or prophesying disgraces her head, for it is one and the same as the woman whose head is shaved. . . . [H]ave her cover her head.

One must wonder that Paul would have such grave concerns over a simple covering worn on one's head, when earlier in the letter he'd stated: "Circumcision is nothing, and uncircumcision is nothing, but what matters is the keeping of the commandments of God" (1 Cor. 7:19). Would Paul consider a mere head covering more important (by reason of requirement) than circumcision?

Both circumcision and head coverings are external; God is interested in the heart. It was time for the Corinthians to reassess what mattered to God and put their ideas of spiritual superiority (men over women) aside. Later Paul states that a woman's hair is her covering, which is also perplexing when put side by side with these statements.

Paul then reiterates their rationale for head coverings in verses 7–9:

> For a man should not have his head covered, since he is the image and glory of God; but the woman is the glory of man. For man does not originate from woman, but woman from man; for indeed man was not created for the woman's sake, but woman for the man's sake.

---

the Son," purported in modern times by theologians like Wayne Grudem and Bruce Ware. This same doctrine was originally suggested in the early centuries of the church and was struck down by church leaders at that time as heresy.

14. Payne, *Man and Woman*, 135.

Why would Paul say man is the image and glory of God, but woman is for the glory of men? Genesis 1:27 states very clearly that both man and woman were created in God's image. Both were charged to be fruitful and to subdue the earth. Together they were to represent God to the world, both reflecting his image.

In light of these perplexities, it is hard to assume the first half of the chiasm are things that Paul believed. Rather, it makes the most sense that these were statements (or questions) the Corinthians had previously written to him.

Now he answers their statements with verses 11–12. He begins: "*However, in the Lord . . .*" Paul is now correcting the Corinthian statements with the truth:

> Neither is woman independent of man, nor is man independent of woman. For as the woman originated from the man, so also the man has his birth through the woman; and all things originate from God.

Rather than suggest a hierarchy as the Corinthians assumed, Paul seems to be *equating* women and men. They share the same source of origin: God himself. They are dependent on each other. No one is above the other.

Then Paul concludes with verse 13:

> Judge for yourselves: is it proper for a woman to pray to God with her head uncovered?

Paul has never been shy about directly addressing matters like the gospel being perverted or salvation through grace alone. But here, he leaves the decision to the Corinthians. Would he have done so if it was an important truth? At the beginning and end of this passage, Paul identifies what's in between as "traditions" or "practices." This is no doctrinal statement. Then what is Paul's point with this chiasm?

Remember his unity theme before and after 11:2–16. Women were being required to wear a head covering by the men because of an incorrect understanding. For the reasons they listed above, men were assumed to be higher than women and were differentiating women by demanding that they keep their heads covered. (In light of the societal norms at the time, it is no surprise this made sense to them.)

But with his response, Paul blows their bad assumptions out of the water. In yet another matter, the Corinthians were completely out of line. He contradicts their incorrect rationales with bold statements about what men and women have in common. Once again, he is promoting a sense of equality and its ensuing unity.

Paul knew they needed to build a community based on love, selflessness, and the equal worth of every member.[15] Any idea or value that caused separation in the body was not from God. Jesus wanted unity for his church, not a hierarchy or division between the haves and the have-nots (see John 17:20–21). No longer were they to be driven by personal rivalries or self-interest. In all matters, they were to work for the common good. As members of his body, men and women were to function as one.[16]

Good News for Today

At the church we attended when our kids were teens, we were blessed with a wonderful youth director. She was a single woman in her late twenties, the kind of person who brings the party with her. All four of my kids adored her—she was all about fun in their activities, but when it came to the Word of God, she was absolutely serious. She met weekly with the teens in our living room, cultivating a bond between her and the kids as well as among each other.

A new young couple began to attend our church and almost immediately expressed an interest in the youth ministry. Our leader welcomed them with open arms and warmly included them into all the activities. But it wasn't long before they seemed to be elbowing

15. Garland, *1 Corinthians*, 6.
16. Garland, *1 Corinthians*, 15.

her out, inserting themselves into the program at the expense of her leadership. She went to the pastor to ask him what to do. She came out of that meeting disillusioned. "Basically, because I am a woman, I am not the leader of choice," she told me. "I got the feeling from him that any man with a pulse would be better than me."

We were heartbroken when she finally called it quits. So were our children. To this day, I wish I had spoken up for her. The thing that sickens me most is how she was treated after pouring herself into those teens for years. She was cast aside without a thought.

Paul's overriding issue pervades through each example he cites in the second half of his letter: the church needs to be a unified body, always choosing to treat each other with love and respect. Unity like that is only possible in a kingdom where women and men share the same worth and privileges.

In the church, when we position one gender above another, we are creating an imbalance in what God designed for equality. We are failing to follow Jesus's instructions and example in relinquishing positions of power and privileges to become servants of all (see Matt. 20:26–27). This was not what Paul or the other apostles endorsed.

Aberrant attitudes concerning male power and authority are just one more way God's description of life in a sinful world at the fall is evident today. It's rather ironic that anyone would embrace male dominance in the very community where sin's control and power has been defeated, in the one place where people have been set free.

To understand how erroneous it is to elevate one gender over the other, we can just look at the damage it causes. Forbidding females from leadership or teaching marginalizes half the church. We are operating without the wisdom and perception of women who have been gifted by the Holy Spirit to function according to their gift-ings, when God considers each of them significant members in the body.

Worse, abusers of that power can lord it over women in the church and home. As Jimmy Carter wrote: "If potential male exploiters of women are led to believe that their victim is considered inferior or 'different' even by God, they can presume that it must be permissible to take advantage of their superior status."[17]

In recent years, the #metoo and #churchtoo movements on social media have yielded scores of women who are finally telling their stories. Before now, they were shamed if they broke silence about what they endured at the hands of abusers in the church and home. They were told to submit, pray for their abuser, and forgive. Male power was God-ordained, after all. Conversely, abusers were generally protected (rather than called out) from consequences for their blatantly sinful behavior. It is a case of incorrect interpretation gone bad.

God designed the church to function in a way that would make this kind of abuse of power unacceptable. It was to be a body where mutual submission and respect were the norm, where the "weak" and the "strong" would have the same kind of care for each other (see 1 Cor. 12:24–25). Someone proclaiming the authority to lord it over others should be an instant red flag to those in the body of Christ.

We are all created in the image of God. There are some who claim that while we are equal in value, we are called to different roles. "In reality, it is simply impossible for women and men to be equal when the man is given intrinsic authority over the woman in a relationship and deemed primary or sole decision-maker."[18]

Our ideas of different roles, one gender over another, must be compared to Genesis 1:28, where both man and woman were commanded to rule and subdue the earth, not each other. They were to do that side by side, as equals. Any deviation from that view of women is a result of the fall, when sin entered creation and perverted God's original design.

As a church, we must exemplify what Jesus (and later Paul) taught about how the body of Christ should function. Women should no

---

17. Jimmy Carter, *A Call to Action: Women, Religion, Violence, and Power* (New York: Simon & Schuster, 2014), 19.
18. Haley Horton, "The Undeniable Link Between Patriarchal Theology and Spiritual Abuse," *CBE International* (blog), January 13, 2021, accessed November 23, 2021, https://www.cbeinternational.org/resource/article/mutuality-blog-magazine /unavoidable-link-between-patriarchal-theology-and.

longer be treated as less than in certain areas of spiritual giftedness. Every person should be encouraged to maturity and growth with no regard to their gender. Every person should be empowered to follow what they believe is God's call on their lives. There is nothing biblical about men governing women. It is seriously unbefitting behavior for the church of Jesus Christ.

Chapter 7

Are Spiritual Gifts Limited by Gender?

Now there are varieties of gifts, but the same Spirit. And there are varieties of ministries, and the same Lord. There are varieties of effects, but the same God who works all things in all persons. But to each one is given the manifestation of the Spirit for the common good. . . . But one and the same Spirit works all these things, distributing to each one individually just as He wills.

—1 Corinthians 12:4–7, 11

For the one who speaks in a tongue does not speak to people, but to God; for no one understands, but in his spirit he speaks mysteries. But the one who prophesies speaks to people for edification, exhortation, and consolation. The one who speaks in a tongue edifies himself; but the one who prophesies edifies the church. . . .

When you assemble, each one has a psalm, has a teaching, has a revelation, has a tongue, has an interpretation. All things are to be done for edification. If anyone speaks in a tongue, it must be by two or at the most three, and each one in turn, and one is to interpret; but if there is no interpreter, he is to keep silent in church; and have him speak to himself and to God. Have two or three prophets speak, and have the others pass judgment. But if a revelation is made to another who is seated, then the first one is to keep silent. For you can all prophesy one by one, so that all may learn and all may be exhorted;

111

and the spirits of prophets are subject to prophets; for God is not a God of confusion, but of peace.

As in all the churches of the saints, the women are to keep silent in the churches; for they are not permitted to speak, but are to subject themselves, just as the Law also says. If they desire to learn anything, let them ask their own husbands at home; for it is improper for a woman to speak in church. Or was it from you that the word of God first went out? Or has it come to you only? . . .

Therefore, my brothers and sisters, earnestly desire to prophesy, and do not forbid speaking in tongues. But all things must be done properly and in an orderly way.

—1 Corinthians 14:2–4, 26–36, 39–40

Focus on 1 Corinthians 12–14

Because she was raised to believe women were not to preach, my friend Julie was more than a little perplexed when, at age fifteen, she began to feel drawn to the pulpit. It didn't make sense that God would call her to something she wasn't allowed to do. She kept her growing desire to herself, assuming it most likely came from her own heart and not from the Lord.

But then one Sunday, out of the blue, at the end of the service, a church deacon walked by. He unexpectedly stopped before her. "You would make a great preacher," he told her. Then he walked on. Hope suddenly rose in her heart. Maybe her burning desire was from God after all!

But then the man stopped, turned around, and added, "It's a shame you're a girl." He moved on, a smile on his face, evidently thinking he had just blessed her with a high compliment. But for Julie, it felt more like he had sucker-punched her in the stomach.

Scripture tells us that every believer is endowed with a gift from the Holy Spirit, so that each person has something to contribute to the church. But does he differentiate between women and men, reserving the gifts of preaching, pastoring, and leadership for males only?

To answer that question, we need to go further into 1 Corinthians, chapters 12 and 14, where Paul offers profound teaching on the spiritual gifts. He has just finished (in 1 Corinthians 11) addressing the Corinthians' divisive behavior during group worship. He'd exhorted them to stop delineating between rich and poor, slave and free, by the haves eating the fellowship meal before the have-nots could get there. With indignation, Paul demands that they stop giving deferential treatment to a select few.

Now, as chapter 12 begins, Paul continues his assault on their disunity from another angle. The Corinthians were placing a higher value on some spiritual gifts (and the people who had them) over others. It was just another line in the same song: giving status to some in the body while completely neglecting the rest.

What Do Spiritual Gifts Have to Do with Unity in the Church?

Every believer is indwelt by the Holy Spirit. His presence is the new Spirit within us, bringing life where there was only death (see Eph. 1:13–14; 4:30; 1 Peter 3:18). He is a permanent guide, there to teach, strengthen, and transform us (see John 14:26; 16:13; 2 Cor. 3:18). His presence is a guarantee of our eternal salvation to come.

The Holy Spirit has also gifted each believer with a special, supernatural ability to be utilized in service to the body. Those gifts vary widely from person to person, and are not given as a merit reward, but through God's grace (undeserved favor). We don't get to choose our gifts—he does, in keeping with his master plan and purposes. Our particular gifts are given according to his will, his wisdom, and his goodness.

Paul explained:

> Now there are varieties of gifts, but the same Spirit. And there are varieties of ministries, and the same Lord. There are varieties of effects, but the same God who works all things in all persons. But to each one is given the manifestation of the Spirit for the common good. . . . But one and the same Spirit works all these things, distributing to each one individually just as He wills. (1 Cor. 12:4–7, 11)

Since all are gifted, without exception, every person is significant and has something to contribute to the body of Christ. No one person can do all the things! Paul likened the Spirit's distribution of gifts to an actual physical body. There are many members, various extremities and organs, all mutually dependent and operating together as one organism.

Every gift is to be used for the edification and building up of the other individuals in the church.[1] They are not for our own self-esteem or to be used in a way that will give one superiority over another. They are for the *common* good (see 1 Cor. 12:7).

In short, we were designed to need each other. This kind of inter-dependence was vividly illustrated in a fable told by Agrippa Menenius to his soldiers.[2] The various parts of a body decided that while they might be working hard to feed the stomach, it was doing nothing for them in return. They collectively agreed to starve the stomach. It wasn't long before fatigue set in for all of them without the nourish-ment the stomach usually provided. Through their folly, they learned the stomach not only had an important purpose, but that none of them could function without it.[3]

As Paul wrote, "The eye cannot say to the hand, 'I have no need of you'; or again, the head to the feet, 'I have no need of you.' . . . But God has so composed the body . . . that there may be no division . . . but that the parts may have the same care for one another" (1 Cor. 12:21, 24–25).

In fact, according to Paul, the members of the body should be so closely bonded, that if one member suffers, the others will suffer along with them. If one member is honored, the others will celebrate with joy (see 12:26). The body of Christ is the ultimate team, where many operate as one toward a common goal. No one person is to be regarded above the rest. Every contribution matters.

The Corinthians hadn't yet conformed to that kingdom principle. Some had been acting as if they were better than the others, because they believed their spiritual gifts (in particular, speaking in tongues)

---

1. Paul urged Timothy, "Do not neglect the spiritual gift within you. . . . Pay close attention to yourself and to the teaching; persevere in these things, for as you do this you will save both yourself and those who hear you" (1 Tim. 4:14, 16). Our gifts are meant to be used in service, not kept to ourselves.
2. The Roman historian Livy recorded this in 494 BC in an effort to obtain accord between the patricians and the plebians.
3. Alice Mathews, *Gender Roles and the People of God: Rethinking What We Were Taught about Men and Women in the Church* (Grand Rapids: Zondervan, 2017), 121.

were far superior to the rest. Those who did not speak in tongues were made to feel inferior, or even envious of those who could.

Why Would the Corinthians Believe That Speaking in Tongues Made Them Superior?

The ability to speak in unknown languages was not limited to the Corinthian church. There were other groups, members of the so-called mystery religions, who for centuries had spoken in strange tongues.[4] The Roman god Apollo, for instance, was believed to be a source of ecstatic utterances. The Oracle of Delphi, who operated out of the Temple of Apollo (near Corinth), was known for this and was considered to be one of the most powerful women in the world.[5] This is just one of the many pagan religions from which newly converted Corinthians had come.

The pagans believed ecstatic utterances were from a god, who entered and took control of the person's body, speaking through that person.[6] Therefore, considering tongues as a sign of great spirituality would have been a natural assumption for new converts. To them, it would have signified those who were closest to God.

But the kingdom of God was far different than the other religions. In Corinth, there seemed to be no concern for the body of worshipers as a whole; members were all about their own personal experience. Paul firmly reinforced the truth that any spiritual gift was strictly for the edification of the fellowship, and not for a single individual's gain.

---

4. The great need during the time of Paul was for salvation; men and women were eager for communion with the divine. Ecstatic utterances were a part of the mystery religions to get them there. Plato mentions this as a phenomenon in his time (437–429 BC). Those who were able to speak in utterances were under divine possessiom. Mortimer J. Adler, *Great Books of the Western World, Volume 3* (Edinburgh: Encyclopedia Britannica Inc., 1952); and Vincent Bridges, "Paganism in Provence," *Journal of the Western Mystery Tradition,* vol. 1, no. 6 (2004).
5. Shane M. Kraeger, "Toward a Mediating Understanding of Tongues: A Historical and Exegetical Examination of Early Literature." *Eleutheria* vol. 1, no. 1 (2010), https://digitalcommons.liberty.edu/eleu/vol1/iss1/5.
6. Leon Morris, *1 Corinthians,* The Tyndale New Testament Commentaries (Grand Rapids: Eerdmans, 1985), 162.

What Did the Early Church Do When They Gathered to Worship?

Most churches today conduct services that follow a plan. Music is chosen beforehand. In some denominations, the churches follow an annual schedule of Bible texts to be taught. If not, pastors have their own plans mapped out. Prayers or recitations are scheduled as well as responsive readings. Not much comes as a surprise on Sunday mornings for most of us; each service follows a predictable routine.

While these things are a part of our modern-day church culture, read how Paul describes the first-century church at Corinth: "When you assemble, each one has a psalm, has a teaching, has a revelation, has a tongue, has an interpretation. All things are to be done for edification" (1 Cor. 14:26). Rather than a rigidly scheduled program, the Corinthians evidently came together and simply waited for the Holy Spirit to lead. But the goal was clear: it was for edifying one another. People shared what God had put on their hearts, maybe requesting a song, reading a passage of Scripture, giving a word from the Lord, or praying aloud. All was to be done in the interest of worship, edification for all, and bringing glory to the Lord Jesus Christ.

While no doubt inspiring and encouraging, this free-flowing model also had a potential for disorder. In Corinth, people were talking, maybe even shouting, over one another. No one was taking turns or willing to yield the floor once they had it, feeling what they had to say was more important than the rest. The Corinthian assembly had been reduced to a cacophony of voices, all vying for attention. Who could understand anything while such disorder ensued?

Paul urged them to change their ways, "for God is not a God of confusion but of peace, as in all the churches of the saints," he told them (14:33 NASB1995). Other congregations were not having difficulty in this regard. No doubt the Corinthians' trouble stemmed from their desire to rise above each other, as expressed in other places in this epistle (see pages 98–100 of this book). Each one was competing for top-dog status, and they were willing to step on the backs of "the competition" to get ahead. (So much for teamwork!)

In the context of all this, Paul makes a perplexing statement: "The women are to keep silent in the churches; for they are not permitted to speak, but are to subject themselves, just as the Law also says" (14:34).

Was Paul Telling Women to Keep Silent for All Time?

"If they desire to learn anything, let them ask their own husbands at home; for it is improper for a woman to speak in church" (14:35).

In my former denomination, 1 Corinthians 14:34–35 was followed quite literally. Women were not permitted to verbally participate in any way (other than singing) in assembly gatherings. Of course, that meant no preaching or teaching, but the restriction went beyond the pulpit. During prayer meetings, women met separately from the men, so both genders could be free to participate. Even in church business meetings, while women were expected to attend, they were not to contribute to the conversation. We sat in silence, just as Paul said we should.

I didn't question this interpretation of Paul's instruction until I was an adult. It was at a Christian conference's morning Bible study. I knew the teacher and was excited to hear his teaching again. He began the first session by inviting questions and input—confirming that in this informal setting, interaction was not just allowed, but encouraged. But then he dropped one last caveat: if you were a woman and had a question or a comment, you should write it out for your husband to read aloud. If you did not have a husband with you, you should flag down one of the runners, who waited to take your written question to the speaker. He would then read it for the group to hear.

I have to confess that I inwardly did some serious eye-rolling! First off, what was the difference between a written note and a verbal expression? In both cases, the words still originated from a woman. Second, what did this policy reveal about their interest in hearing from their women outside of a formal worship meeting? Was there no place where women could converse with men about the Word of

God, like Mary of Bethany did with the twelve disciples at the feet of Jesus?

As the session went on, I did think of a question, as well as several comments. But I saved them until the session was over. I walked down the aisle to the teacher. "I do have a couple of comments," I confessed, "but I just couldn't bring myself to flag down a runner. It was just too demeaning. And not at all how Jesus handled women in public places."

He nodded sadly in agreement. "So sorry about that," he apologized. "I wasn't given a choice as to how this study should be conducted."

Was this conference policy a valid application of what Paul wrote on the silence of women? Not if you take the immediate context of his words into consideration.

Remember, there was confusion and discord during the assembly meetings in Corinth. Paul addressed that distressing situation by offering three examples of people who were not considering the needs of the group, but only themselves when it came to their participation in the gathering.

1. The first example concerned those who practiced speaking in tongues during the service. Paul told them: "If anyone speaks in a tongue, it must be by two or at the most three, and each one in turn, and one is to interpret; but if there is no interpreter, he is to keep silent in church; and have him speak to himself and to God" (1 Cor. 14:27–28). There was only one valid reason to practice your gift in a group setting: to edify the entire church. If the speaker was the only one who would benefit, he should keep his peace.

2. The prophets were also under Paul's scrutiny. Some were apparently monopolizing the spotlight and not ceding the platform to others who had a prophecy to share. "Have two or three prophets speak, and have the others pass judgment," Paul wrote in verse 29. Prophets were to listen to each other, to discern that their colleagues' contributions lined up with

what they knew Scripture said. But some were so intent on getting to say their piece that important responsibility was being neglected.

"But if a revelation is made to another who is seated," Paul added, "the first one is to keep silent. For you can all prophesy one by one, so that all may learn and all may be exhorted; and the spirits of prophets are subject to prophets" (14:30–32).

It seems that the prophets in Corinth were "hogging the mic." Once they had everyone's attention, it was hard to yield the floor. So they kept talking, even when another prophet was obviously waiting to share what the Lord had given them.

Paul later expressed his sentiment for this kind of behavior in his letter to the Philippians: "Do nothing from selfishness or empty conceit, but with humility consider one another as more important than yourselves; do not merely look out for your own personal interests, but also for the interests of others" (Phil. 2:3–4). Neither self-importance nor exclusion has a place in the kingdom. We are to follow our Savior's example of humility and love. When it's all about us, it's not about God.

3. Paul gave one final example from the chaos that reigned in their assembly. "Women are to keep silent in the churches; for they are not permitted to speak, but are to subject themselves, just as the Law also says. If they desire to learn anything, let them ask their own husbands at home; for it is improper for a woman to speak in church" (1 Cor. 14:34–35).

Before we can understand what Paul was saying with these verses, we need to know a bit more. First of all, *keep silent* is an interpretation for the Greek verb *sigao*, which can also be translated "to say nothing, keep still" or "to hold one's peace."[7] A look at the other contexts in the New Testament that contain this word gives us a broader perspective:

---

7. BDAG, *sigao*, 922.

- It is used of the disciples, after witnessing the Transfiguration, who kept quiet about what they saw until the appropriate time for it to be revealed (see Luke 9:36; 20:26).

- It describes what a talkative crowd did when a disciple waved for their attention and began to speak. The people stopped talking in order to listen (see Acts 12:17; 15:12).

- It refers to God's withholding a revelation of the mystery of the gospel, "kept secret for long ages past" (Rom. 16:25). The mystery was withheld for only a time, until Christ came to earth. We can now know God's gospel and plan for the world, as revealed in the New Testament.

Here is something important to note: Paul asks for *sigao* from *all three examples* in 1 Corinthians 14. He tells the tongue speakers to be silent in 14:28, the prophets to be silent in 14:30, and women to be silent in 14:34. Yet, when I have heard this passage taught, only the third example (women) is portrayed as a rule for all time. No one seems to give much thought to the fact that Paul has commanded prophets and tongue speakers to be silent as well. However, in every example, Paul asks for silence for a time, until it is appropriate to share what they have to say for the meeting. In each example, Paul's reason for requesting their silence is a temporary concern that can be successfully addressed.

Another thing that can add to our understanding is the first-century cultural expectations for a lecture setting. It was standard practice for a speaker to respond to intermittent questions as he taught.[8] Those in the audience who were somewhat informed were encouraged to interact with the speaker's presentation. However, novices in the group knew to stay quiet; it was considered rude for the ignorant to interrupt the proceedings.[9] (A modern-day equivalent is

---

8. Craig S. Keener, "Learning in the Assemblies: 1 Corinthians 14:34–35," in *Discovering Biblical Equality: Complementarity Without Hierarchy*, ed. Ronald W. Pierce, Rebecca Merrill Groothuis, and Gordon D. Fee (Downers Grove, IL: IVP Academic, 2005), 165.

9. Craig Keener, *The IVP Bible Background Commentary: New Testament* (Downers Grove, IL: InterVarsity Press, 1993), 483.

in the Bible Study Fellowship organization. Until recently, students in discussion groups were asked to refrain from contributing if they had not done the homework beforehand. This was so the group could avoid deviations away from the passage.)

Women in the first century were far less trained in both the Scriptures and public reasoning than were men.[10] It could be that in their enthusiasm to be included in the discussion, they were peppering the instructor with so many questions that they were becoming a distraction to the group. Paul, then, is urging women to hold their peace until they can get some preliminary schooling from their husbands at home. Until they knew enough to enter the discussion intelligently, they should remain quiet.

This interpretation fits with Paul's other two examples. All three groups (tongue speakers, prophets, and certain women) were monopolizing center stage and edifying themselves at the expense of the group. Each of them was more concerned about their personal needs and desires than they were about the other church members present.

As a remedy, Paul advised that the women "play catch-up" at home. But silence was not a permanent restriction. Paul actually warned Timothy about the false teachers who desired women to remain in a perpetual learning status: "For among them are those who slip into households and captivate weak women weighed down with sins, led on by various impulses, *always learning and never able to come to the knowledge of the truth*" (2 Tim. 3:6–7, emphasis mine).[11] In light of this, it stands to reason that once women knew enough to add to the discussion with their questions, they would be welcome to participate, and use their informed contributions to strengthen the church.

There is one more concept Paul communicates to these three groups: their need for submission (Greek: *hypotasso*[12]). While many

---

10. Keener, *IVP Bible Background Commentary: New Testament*, 483.
11. We also read in Heb. 6:1: "Therefore leaving the elementary teaching about the Christ, let us press on to maturity."
12. The Greek verb *hypotasso* is discussed at length on pages 158–159 of this book. Translators in various versions of the Bible use the verb "to submit" or " to be subject to."

restrict this word to mean one person bowing to another's authority, its meaning here is much more significant and involves the entire Christian community. In Ephesians 5:21, Paul urges his readers: ". . . subject yourselves to one another in the fear of Christ." Obviously not everyone can be an authority to everyone else. Mutual submission must mean more.[13]

A better understanding of submission can be found in Jesus's example. "Have this attitude in yourselves which was also in Christ Jesus, who, as He already existed in the form of God, did not consider equality with God a thing to be grasped, but emptied Himself, taking the form of a bond-servant and being born in the likeness of men" (Phil. 2:5–7). He left his glory for the sake of sinners who needed pardon and restoration, sacrificing himself for the good of humankind. While the word *submit* is not explicitly mentioned, Jesus's spirit of submission to the Father when coming to earth is quite obvious.

Paul's and Peter's unusual view of submission in leadership came from Jesus himself: "You know that the rulers of the Gentiles lord it over them, and *their* great men exercise authority over them. It is not this way among you, but whoever wishes to become great among you shall be your servant, and whoever wishes to be first among you shall be your slave; just as the Son of Man did not come to be served, but to serve, and to give His life a ransom for many" (Matt. 20:25–28 NASB1995, emphasis mine).

Nor did Paul consider himself above the others. He viewed himself as least of all the apostles and foremost among sinners (1 Cor. 15:9; 1 Tim. 1:15). Peter echoed the need for humility when he told the elders of the churches to "shepherd the flock of God among you, exercising oversight, not under compulsion but voluntarily, according to the will of God; and not with greed but with eagerness; *nor yet as domineering over those assigned to your care, but by proving to be examples* to the flock" (1 Peter 5:2–3, emphasis mine).

---

13. See chapter 9, pages 158–161, for more on submission.

When kingdom citizens submit (*hypotasso*) to each other, they put themselves aside for the sake of others. Let's look at how Paul applied the idea of submission to his three examples in 1 Corinthians 14:

1. To those speaking in tongues, he urged thinking past their own desires to what would edify everyone else. While he did not use the specific word *submit*, the spirit of the word is most certainly demonstrated here.

2. As he turns his attention to the prophets, Paul did use the word *submit* when he said the spirits of the prophets submit to prophets. Again, he is asking them to yield the floor to each other and treat the others as more important than themselves. They are to listen to each other's input, not just communicate their own.

3. Then, in his final example, Paul asks the women to refrain from asking questions until they can positively contribute to the teaching. For a third time, he asks a group to *submit*, or give up on what might be of personal benefit for the sake of the body.

In short, choosing to interpret 1 Corinthians 14:34–35 as a command for all women for all time to remain silent in the church takes Paul's request out of its context and assigns a meaning Paul did not communicate in the rest of what he said.

Unity necessitates being a team player: considering each teammate a significant and equal part of the group. This means wanting what's best for each one, suffering as they suffer, rejoicing at their victories, and working in tandem to keep the body functioning as it should. This includes holding your tongue when what you have to say or ask will not benefit the whole body, regardless of your gender.

Are There Any Gender Qualifications or Limitations in the Exercising of Spiritual Gifts?

There are four places in the New Testament where Paul lists spiritual gifts.

Romans 12:6–8	1 Corinthians 12:4–10	1 Corinthians 12:27–29	Ephesians 4:7–12
To the church in Rome	To the church in Corinth	To the church in Corinth	To the church in Ephesus
Since we have gifts that differ according to the grace given to us, each of us is to use them properly . . .	But to each one is given the manifestation of the Spirit for the common good. . . .	Now you are Christ's body, and individually parts of it. And God has appointed . . .	But to each one of us grace was given according to the measure of Christ's gift. . . .
Prophecy Service Teaching Exhortation Giving Leading Mercy	Word of Wisdom Word of Knowledge Faith Healing Miracle Working Prophecy Discerning of spirits Tongues Interpretation of tongues	Apostles Prophets Teachers Miracle Workers Healers Helpers Administrators Speakers of tongues	Apostles Prophets Evangelists Pastors Teachers

As you can see, each list varies from one to the other. Few of the gifts are on all four lists. The Holy Spirit assigns gifts according to the needs of the body, which may differ from congregation to congregation.[14] For these reasons, I believe it is safe to assume what Paul listed in these four passages is not exhaustive.

---

14. In Paul's letter to the Romans, the gifts are from the Father, and in Ephesians, they are from the Son. Here in 1 Corinthians, the gifts are given by the Spirit. The whole Trinity is involved in the distribution of gifts.

It is important to note that none of the gifts listed are qualified by gender. Paul wrote to the entire congregation, both male and female. Also, none of the gifts are qualified by a person's economic status or racial background. Believers who are rich, poor, slaves, masters, Jews, and Gentiles all receive spiritual gifts within the body without regard to these identifiers (Gal. 3:28). Why not also without regard to gender?

Given the inclusive nature of Paul's writing here, if there were gender restrictions, he would have mentioned them. Instead, we see the first list in 1 Corinthians 12 qualified with "each one." No indicator of gender is attached to any of the gifts on any list. (You may be wondering at this point about 1 Timothy 2:12, where Paul writes "I do not allow a woman to teach." We will cover that passage in the next chapter.)

Remember, Paul has already clarified some matters of gender in both chapters 7 and 11. This would be a perfect opportunity for him to keep limitations straight, continuing gender issues into this chapter. Yet he does not bring it into the discussion when it comes to spiritual gifts.

We've already seen that the gift of prophecy was being exercised by both men and women in 1 Corinthians 11:5, 13. Paul gives no indication that this is a problem. So, as Paul instructed those speaking in tongues and prophesying to hold their peace, he was addressing men and women alike. To assume that women were not qualified to participate verbally is to read something into the passage that does not exist.

Good News for Today

Sadly, there are many women afraid to exercise their spiritual gifts within the church. Those fears are not unfounded; many women who cross traditional interpretations of Scripture have been shamed publicly or privately.

For example, my friend Rosa has been blessed by God with a successful radio and writing ministry. She has interviewed some of the best-known names in Christianity. But her notoriety has attracted the inevitable haters. They believe that she is in direct disobedience to Scripture by having a vocal ministry as a woman. On one particular post, Rosa received over 1,300 angry, curse word–laden comments and personal messages decrying her as a heretic, a Jezebel spirit, and other similarly cruel things. "Christians," she told me, "have treated me like garbage. I could not have a more night-and-day experience between the world and my Christian 'brethren.'"

Billy Graham has said that his daughter Anne is the most gifted preacher of all his children. Early in her ministry, Anne Graham Lotz was asked to speak for a statewide convention of pastors. As she took the podium, many of the eight hundred pastors present stood and turned their chairs around, facing their backs toward her. Anne writes, "When I concluded my message, I was shaking. I was hurt and surprised that godly men would find what I was doing so offensive that they would stage such a demonstration, especially when I was an invited guest. For me," she continues, "[being obedient to God's call] means going wherever God sends and giving out His Word to whomever He puts in front of me."[15]

When my friend Stacy became the head pastor for her church, she expected resistance. But what she got was downright frightening. She says, "The harassment and the name-calling intensified. Terrible rumors were being spread about me. My computer was hacked. There were actual threats made to my physical person. I had to wear a bulletproof vest and have security sit in the lobby. My husband even started bringing his gun to church." She continued, "It still makes me sad to think about it. I was just trying to follow God's calling and to love His people."

There are thousands more stories disappointingly similar. A woman obeys God's gifting and call on her life, and her Christian brothers

---

15. Anne Graham Lotz, "Jesus Calls Women to Serve and Lead," *The Washington Post*, September 21, 2008. Copyright © 2021 Anne Graham Lotz (AnGeL Ministries) Raleigh, North Carolina, USA. Used by permission. All rights reserved. www.annegrahamlotz.org.

and sisters attack, intent on destruction. I recently read one blogger, who wrote of a successful female author, "Her husband should love her by telling her to shut up."

It is rather ironic that people claiming to speak in the name of the Lord could be filled with such hate and vitriol. Their self-righteous and destructive intent is eerily similar to the chief priests and Pharisees' reaction to Jesus raising Lazarus from the dead. Rather than accepting the miracle as validation for his claims, their knee-jerk reaction was to fight against it. "Therefore the chief priests and the Pharisees convened a council meeting, and they were saying, 'What are we doing in regard to the fact that this man is performing many signs? If we let Him go on like this, all the people will believe in Him, and the Romans will come and take over both our place and our nation.'" John tells us, "So from that day on they planned together to kill Him" (John 11:47–48, 11:53).

Many angry attempts to dismiss women are rooted in that kind of fear. Church leaders equate women's obeying God's call with secular feminism, claiming this is disobedience to the "authority of Scripture" (i.e., what in reality is their interpretation of certain Scriptures). They warn if this is allowed, the church will quickly fall to liberalism, where the Bible will not be respected or even largely ignored.

But the biblical scholars I have read who find no gender limits also believe all Scripture is the inspired Word of God. They are not questioning the truth or reliability of Scripture. They are questioning human interpretation.

I'm sure Paul would not have approved of the gender war promoted by some. As we saw in the epistle to the Corinthians, Paul didn't view any ministry, whether performed by women or by men, as more or less important than any others. His determination was that the entire church, men and women alike, submit to one another and operate in love. Every person, regardless of gender, has a significant role in the body of Christ.

As I stated earlier, we don't get to choose our gifts. The Holy Spirit endows them according to his will and purpose, to men and women alike. Unfortunately, today's evangelical church is keeping some Holy Spirit–endowed women under its thumb.

Imagine what could happen in the world if every one of us in the church were encouraged to use our gifts for his glory. I was able to see firsthand what this could look like several years ago in my own church. Our pastor received a call to leave our church for a new ministry. Rather than hire an interim pastor, the elders decided to have the congregation take on the responsibilities that were left uncovered. A teaching team was formed to fill the Sunday pulpit. Those gifted in pastoral care, like lay counseling or visitation for the elderly and sick, formed a committee to ensure all those needs were met. When someone came to the elders with an idea for a new ministry, the leadership response was almost always, "How can we help you pursue that?"

Surprisingly, rather than the church faltering with no one "at the helm," we thrived. Concerned for the church's well-being after the pastor departed, many "pew sitters" suddenly became active in serving. A new energy filled the place. You could sense it just walking in the door on a Sunday morning. As people were encouraged to use their gifts, they became personally invested in the church's ministry, no longer there to merely receive, but to give. No one person was burdened with the load (as pastors commonly are); it was so much healthier than making our church a one-man show. It is the way God designed us to operate: every member contributing, every member significant to the body, and each one submitting to the other as Paul called us to do. Disputes or division tend to disappear when we work as a team toward a common goal. That means supporting each other in the responsibilities we are called to fill. When we yield to the Spirit, the church is transformed.

Chapter 8

Should Women Be Allowed to Teach Men?

Therefore I want the men in every place to pray, lifting up holy hands, without anger and dispute. Likewise, I want women to adorn themselves with proper clothing, modestly and discreetly, not with braided hair and gold or pearls or expensive apparel, but rather by means of good works, as is proper for women making a claim to godliness. A woman must quietly receive instruction with entire submissiveness. But I do not allow a woman to teach or to exercise authority over a man, but to remain quiet. For it was Adam who was first created, and then Eve. And it was not Adam who was deceived, but the woman was deceived and became a wrongdoer. But women will be preserved through childbirth—if they continue in faith, love, and sanctity, with moderation.

—1 Timothy 2:8–15

Focus on 1 Timothy 2:11–15

When our pastor went on sabbatical years ago, the elders decided to use those in the body gifted to teach to fill the pulpit. As they discussed who to include, our pastor advised, "Be sure to tap Julie Coleman. She's a natural." When the elders approached me, I was thrilled. But I was also a little uncomfortable. What about 1 Timothy 2, where Paul forbids women to teach? They assured me: I wasn't usurping authority from men. The elders were *asking* me to do it.

I had a shiny new seminary degree and had begun writing in earnest. For many years, I had been teaching women in Bible studies and at retreats. Teaching came to me as easily as breathing. Yet this new opportunity seemed so . . . different. Standing at the podium? Preaching to men? I wasn't so sure I was doing the right thing.

On the morning of my first sermon, as I stood for a sound check before the service, an elder walked by the platform. "You might want to step back a few paces," I warned him, half tongue-in-cheek. "In case I get struck by lightning."

As I continued sharing that ministry with the other three teaching team members, I became more and more comfortable with the opportunity the Lord had provided for me to use my gift. But that one verse in 1 Timothy continued to trouble me.

I wasn't alone. That fall, I asked our women's Bible study if we could study 1 Timothy. I knew I had to get to the bottom of the issue, because as much as I loved preaching, I didn't want to be doing anything that the Lord did not want me to do. The women readily agreed. They wanted to settle the issue for themselves as well. We dug in.

In a few months, we arrived at *the* passage, where Paul began, "I do not allow a woman to teach or exercise authority over a man, but to remain quiet" (1 Tim. 2:12). Our study attendance doubled that week; my living room was filled to capacity and overflowed into the dining room. It felt like we were collectively holding our breath, anxious to hear what the Lord would reveal.

First Timothy 2 has its challenges. Like in 1 Corinthians 11, scholars differ widely in their interpretation of Paul's words. In fact, even those who agree about whether women should preach or not differ from each other when interpreting the details.

There are questions related to v. 12 that raise important issues.

1. Paul tells women to receive instruction quietly and to remain quiet. But in 1 Corinthians 11, he has no problem with women prophesying or praying aloud in the body. Is 1 Timothy in conflict with his earlier instruction?

2. Is Paul instructing all women to be perpetual students? In 2 Timothy 3:7, he warns against women "always learning and never able to come to the knowledge of the truth."[1] How can these be reconciled?

3. A controversy revolves around the verb *authenteo*, translated (in the New American Standard Bible) as *usurping authority*. The problem is that this verb only occurs once in the entire New Testament. In fact, even in the secular writings of the first century, it is only found two other times.[2] How can we be sure we have accurately understood its meaning?

4. Apart from this verse, there are no instructions in the New Testament that specifically limit women from teaching/preaching. Since a limitation like that would impact half of all believers, why didn't Paul bring it up in any of his other letters?

---

1. Also, "For though by this time you ought to be teachers, you have need again for someone to teach you the elementary principles of the actual words of God, and you have come to need milk and not solid food. . . . But solid food is for the mature, who because of practice have their senses trained to distinguish between good and evil" (Heb. 5:12, 14).

2. Lucy Peppiatt, *Rediscovering Scripture's Vision for Women* (Downers Grove, IL: InterVarsity Press, 2019), 150.

Many view all other passages pertinent to women through the lens of this one verse containing an obscure term (*authenteo*).[3] Some friends recall a conference at a conservative seminary in which this verse was on the table. One of the seminarians spoke up. "Are there any other major doctrines in the Bible which depend on one verse?" He was assured by his professors there were none. "And is it true that the understanding of this verse is dependent upon the translation of just one verb which is used only once in the entire New Testament?"[4]

You have to admit, this is a sticky issue. It is always dangerous to base doctrine on a single, difficult passage, especially when the context is not carefully considered. We must do our due diligence in examining the literary context (the rest of Paul's letter) as well as the historical situation at the time of Paul's writing, and reconcile the passage to the context of the entire New Testament and the Bible. Only then can we hope to accurately interpret what Paul was communicating to his readers.

Why Did Paul Write the Letter?

Paul was writing to Timothy, whom he calls his "son in the faith" in verse 2. Timothy was serving the Lord in the city of Ephesus per Paul's request, in order to, in Paul's words, "instruct certain men not to teach strange doctrines" (1 Tim. 1:3 NASB1995).[5] False teachers were a widespread problem in the early church. In fact, a majority of the books in the New Testament mention the dangers of first-century heresy.[6]

The lack of a complete New Testament and the infrequency of Paul's apostolic visits to the young churches left room for erroneous teaching to make its way into a congregation. Some heresies had great

---

3. Richard Clark Kroeger and Catherine Clark Kroeger, *I Suffer Not a Woman to Teach: Rethinking 1 Timothy 2:11–15 in Light of Ancient Evidence* (Grand Rapids: Baker Academic, 1992), 12.
4. Kroeger and Kroeger, *I Suffer Not a Woman*, 12.
5. NASB1995 translates as "men" but the pronoun here is neutral.
6. More than 20 percent of the Pastoral Epistles deal with false teachers and their erroneous doctrines, in addition to a great deal of instruction on how to set the situation straight (Kroeger and Kroeger, *I Suffer Not a Woman*, 42).

appeal for certain individuals. Paul wrote: "For the time will come when they will not tolerate sound doctrine; but wanting to have their ears tickled, they will accumulate for themselves teachers in accordance with their own desires, and will turn away their ears from the truth and will turn aside to myths" (2 Tim. 4:3–4). The false teachers were leading the Ephesians into a religion of their imaginations. Bits and pieces from pagan cults had (most likely) been melded together into something very different than the gospel that had saved them.

Paul had previously warned the Ephesians about these "savage wolves" who would "come in among you, not sparing the flock; and from among your own selves men will arise, speaking perverse things to draw away the disciples after them" (Acts 20:29–30). Some had already fallen away. Paul names Hymenaeus and Alexander as having been "shipwreck[ed] in regard to their faith" (1 Tim. 1:19–20).

How could people so easily be led away from the truth? It is a human tendency to fall back on that which is familiar and comfortable, even when the familiar is vastly inferior to the new thing we have been given.[7]

According to Paul, the teachers had craftily inserted their heresy into the body. They initiated what Paul called "fruitless discussion" and "empty chatter" (1 Tim. 1:6; 6:20). Myths were told that opposed the Jewish Scriptures, changing details which perverted the truth. As they interacted with the faithful, they stirred up a morbid interest in controversial questions; that controversy had given rise to "envy, strife, abusive language, evil suspicions, and constant friction between people of depraved mind and deprived of the truth" (1 Tim. 6:4–5).

Who were these false teachers? Paul does not identify a specific group. So while we can't derive *who*, we can derive *what* was erroneously being taught from Paul's response in this letter, along with 2 Timothy and Titus.[8]

---

7. As was the case in Exodus, when, after a dramatic rescue out of slavery, at the first sign of trouble, the Israelites begged to go back to Egypt.
8. These three letters, called the Pastoral Epistles, were written to men who were

What Exactly Were the False Teachers Promoting?

The more the false teachers said, the more confusing their content became (see 1 Tim. 6:20). There are many similarities in what Paul says about their false teaching in 1 and 2 Timothy to early Gnosticism.[9] Ancient gnostic writings contain that kind of material, meanings obscured within perplexing riddles and paradoxes. Reading those texts today "can be a frustrating experience because of the deliberate obfuscation in them."[10]

The Gnostics were a religious sect that had its origins in Platonic philosophy in the centuries before Christ.[11] The word *gnostic* is from the Greek *gnosis*, meaning *knowledge*. Gnostics taught that the way to salvation was through hidden, divine knowledge.[12] Gnostics believed only the spiritual world is good; the entire material world is evil and could only have been created by an inferior god (who had to have been either ignorant or evil to produce a material creation). They believed that only the highest god was good.

Concerning humans, the Gnostics believed the physical body and soul are also evil. The only thing redeemable in man is his spirit (which they called the divine spark), which lies trapped in his evil soul. The spirit is asleep and ignorant and can only be awakened and liberated by knowledge. Once the spirit is so enlightened, it could be released and return to be reunited with the highest god. When every spark was finally returned to him, the world would be set right for good.

---

ministering in struggling congregations. First Timothy and Titus are thought to have been written around the same time. Both deal with similar issues. Titus, serving on the island of Crete, is similarly called "my true son in a common faith" by Paul (Titus 1:4).

9. In 1945, a library of ancient gnostic teachings was discovered in Egypt. They are authored by a variety of Gnostics. They give us insight, as many first-century ideas have similarities with gnostic ideas.

10. Kroeger and Kroeger, *I Suffer Not a Woman*, 61.

11. Gnosticism had its roots in Platonic thought, which dates back to about 400 years before Christ. Gnosticism blossomed into a full-blown religion in the second century AD, but at the time of Paul, the early tenets were taking shape and had many followers.

12. The word for "knowledge" in this passage is *gnosis*.

Were there early Gnostics in Ephesus? Yes, there were, according to the book of Revelation. In the first of the letters to the seven churches, Jesus commends the Ephesians: "But you have this, that you hate the deeds of the Nicolaitans, which I also hate" (Rev. 2:6). The church fathers identified the Nicolaitans and their descendants as a branch of Gnosticism.[13]

There's no direct link to prove the teaching of Paul in this letter was directed at early Gnostics. But the cult is worth mentioning, since some of Paul's reasons listed in 1 Timothy 2:13–15 for his prohibition in verse 12 correlate to gnostic tenets. It's also possible that the false teachers had inserted a combination of pagan beliefs into what they were teaching.

Paul also writes of the false teachers' interest in the law, "wanting to be teachers of the Law, even though they do not understand either what they are saying or the matters about which they make confident assertions" (1 Tim. 1:7). Later in the letter, Paul refutes their imposed rules like forbidding marriage, abstaining from certain foods, and unhealthy bodily discipline (see 1 Tim. 4:1–5). They were drawing the Ephesians away from faith in Jesus for their salvation and burdening them with earning their salvation through works. Paul viewed their deception as satanic (see 1 Tim. 4:1).

What Is the Context Surrounding Paul's Instruction on a Woman Teaching?

Earlier in chapter 2, Paul urges the entire congregation to be in prayer on "behalf of all people . . . so that we may lead a tranquil and quiet life in all godliness and dignity" (1 Tim. 2:1–2). He urges "men in every place to pray, lifting up holy hands, without anger and dispute" (2:8).

Then Paul turns to the women: "Likewise, I want women to adorn themselves with proper clothing, modestly and discreetly, not with

---

13. Richard Watson, "Nicolaitans," in *Watson's Biblical & Theological Dictionary*, accessed November 11, 2021, https://www.studylight.org/dictionaries/eng/wtd/n/nicolaitans.html.

braided hair and gold or pearls or expensive apparel, but rather by means of good works, as is proper for women making a claim to godliness" (1 Tim. 2:9–10). Just as the men were to pray without anger and dispute, women were to show their prayerful attitude with their actions.

I believe that Paul is not instructing about literal clothing, but is contrasting the external with the internal. It was not about what they wore, but what was in their hearts. He uses the same metaphoric language in Colossians: "*Put on* the new self, which is being renewed to a true knowledge according to the image of the One who created it . . . *put on* a heart of compassion, kindness, humility, gentleness and patience. . . . In addition to all these things *put on* love. . . . *Let the peace of Christ . . . rule in your hearts.* . . . Whatever you do in word or deed, do everything in the name of the Lord Jesus, giving thanks through Him to God the Father" (3:10, 12, 14–15, 17, emphasis mine). By choosing to align their hearts with the Father (which happens when we pray), the Ephesians would lead "a quiet and tranquil life."

But not all of the women were conducting themselves in that way.

"A woman must quietly receive instruction with entire submissiveness. But I do not allow a woman to teach or exercise authority over a man, but to remain quiet" (1 Tim. 2:11–12). It doesn't always come through in English translations, but Paul starts this section with a plural (women as a whole), switches to a singular person, then ends with a plural pronoun.

vv. 9–10 Likewise, I want *women* [plural] to adorn themselves . . . as is proper for *women* [plural] making a claim to godliness.

v. 11 A *woman* [singular] must quietly receive instruction with entire submissiveness.

v. 12 But I do not allow a *woman* [singular] to teach . . .

v. 15 But *women* [singular *she* in the original Greek] will be preserved through childbirth—if *they* [plural] continue in faith, love, and sanctity, with moderation.

We need to pay attention to Paul's specific choice of pronouns. He chose them for a reason. One interesting possibility is that Paul is singling out a particular woman for her false teaching.[14] His charge to Timothy: she must learn with entire submissiveness (from teachers who would correct the errors in her understanding). She should not be teaching or seeking dominance over those leaders who were proclaiming the truth. Her actions were the opposite of a prayerful, submissive attitude.

After Paul gives this restriction on a woman teaching, he continues, "*For* . . ." This small word is important. It signals he is about to give reasons for that instruction. Here is a bird's-eye view of the things that he lists.

	Implied Content of False Teaching	Known Gnostic Teaching	Paul's Correction
Reason #1	Eve was created before Adam.	Eve was created first and is the mother of all mankind.	"For it was Adam who was first created, and then Eve."
Reason #2	Adam was deceived, not the woman.	Eve is the hero in creation, because she imparted knowledge to Adam.	"And it was not Adam who was deceived, but the woman was deceived and became a wrongdoer."
Reason #3	Women cannot obtain salvation while bearing children.	To bear children was to disseminate the spark of deity within you, entrapping that spark in a soul which is evil.	"But women will be preserved through childbirth —if they continue in faith, love, and sanctity, with moderation."

14. Other passages demonstrate that women were involved in false teaching: 1 Tim. 4:7; 5:11–13; Titus 1:11.

Note the signal words at the beginning of Paul's responses to each false teaching: "for," "and," and "but." It certainly seems Paul was refuting gnostic teaching point by point. Now that we've had a big-picture view, we will look in detail at Paul's rebuttals.

Reason #1: "For it was Adam who was first created, and then Eve."
Many interpret this to mean Adam's position as "firstborn" in the creation account gave him an exalted status over Eve. But this assumption is not supported throughout the context of the rest of Genesis. There were indeed times when God chose a later sibling over the firstborn in personal interaction and in carrying out the family line.[15] One of the natural consequences of the fall was a corruption of the first couple's relationship: that the woman would desire her husband, but he will rule over her (see Gen. 3:16). This was not a curse or imposed punishment, but a description of life in a sinful world. The tyranny of men over women was not God's design. God's design was a perfect harmony between them.[16] Sin is the great destroyer. It corrupted man's pure love into a desire to dominate.

But Jesus rescued us from that oppression, setting us free so that we would no longer live under the slavery of sin (see Rom. 6:8–14). When we believed in him, Jesus pulled us out of the domain of darkness and placed us into his kingdom of light (see Col. 1:13). We are to live in the here and now as citizens of that kingdom (see Phil. 3:20). Part of that is in how we conduct our relationships with each other. We are to live the way God designed us to live before sin ruined it all.

So rather than assuming Paul is teaching a creation-order hierarchy, there is another likely possibility to consider: with this first statement, Paul could well be refuting fraudulent teaching about Eve. The gnostic account of the creation story glorified Eve and the serpent.[17] They believed that Eve was the first human and actually gave life to

---

15. See chapter 1 in this book, specifically note pages 26–27.
16. Again, see chapter 1, noting pages 27–28.
17. Kroeger and Kroeger, *I Suffer Not a Woman*, 21.

Adam.[18] Paul here contradicts that teaching with the true Word of God: God created Adam first, not Eve. The false teaching blatantly changed the truth of Genesis with a distortion.

Another prevalent and perverted doctrine he may have been refuting originated in the pagan worship of Artemis. The city of Ephesus was devoted to Artemis, who was the goddess of hunting, chastity, childbirth, and fertility. She was worshiped all over the Greek world. The temple built in her honor at Ephesus was one of the seven wonders of the ancient world—four times bigger than the Parthenon in Athens! Pilgrim worshipers came from all over the world to pay their respects to her, making the tourist industry a major part of Ephesian economy (see Acts 19:26–28). Eve was eventually equated to Artemis in Gnostic literature, venerated as the mother of all life, including Adam.[19]

In giving truth to contradict what was taught about Eve, Paul is building a case for how contrary the false teachings are to the true Word of God.

Reason #2: "And it was not Adam who was deceived, but the woman was deceived and became a wrongdoer."
We can turn Paul's correction around to deduce what incorrect doctrine (the) woman was teaching—that at the fall, Eve was not the one being deceived. It was Adam who was deceived.

---

18. In the gnostic writing, *The Hypostasis of the Archons*, Adam acknowledges that Eve has given him life:

> The rulers took counsel with one another and said, 'Come, let us cause a deep sleep to fall upon Adam.' And he slept. – Now the deep sleep that they 'caused to fall upon him, and he slept' is Ignorance. – They opened his side like a living woman. And they built up his side with some flesh in place of her, and Adam came to be endowed only with soul.
>
> And the spirit-endowed woman came to him and spoke with him, saying, 'Arise, Adam.' And when he saw her, he said, 'It is you who have given me life; you will be called 'mother of the living'. – For it is she who is my mother. It is she who is the physician, and the woman, and she who has given birth.'

Bentley Layton, trans., "The Hypostasis of the Archons" in *Early Christian Writings*, accessed November 17, 2020, http://www.earlychristianwritings.com /text/archons.html.

19. Kroeger and Kroeger, *I Suffer Not a Woman*, 52.

Interestingly, the Gnostics depicted Eve as the hero in the creation story. She was the imparter of knowledge to Adam, waking his sleeping soul and spiritually enlightening him by offering him the fruit of the Tree of Knowledge.[20] With his second reason for rejecting bad teaching, Paul refutes that erroneous teaching with the Word of God: Eve was no hero, but actually was the first to fall in disobedience to God's command.

Some try to explain Paul's statement by suggesting Paul means that women, by nature, are easily deceived (so they shouldn't be trusted to teach). But there is no indication in the Genesis account of greater gullibility on the part of Eve. She may have held the conversation with the serpent, but both Adam and Eve ate the fruit (see Gen. 3:6).

Some speculate women are being called here to suffer for the sin of Eve; that because she was cursed at the fall, so are her offspring. (One has to wonder why only the female offspring are called to suffer for

---

20. From *The Apocraphon of John*:

> And he sent, through his beneficent Spirit and his great mercy, a helper to Adam, luminous Epinoia which comes out of him, who is called 'Life' [*Zoe*]. And she assists the whole creature, by toiling with him and by restoring him to his fullness and by teaching him about the descent of his seed (and) by teaching him about the way of ascent, (which is) the way he came down.

Later Eve is quoted saying:

> I am the light which exists in the light, I am the remembrance of the Pronoia—that I might enter into the midst of darkness and the inside of Hades. And I filled my face with the light of the completion of their aeon. And I entered into the midst of their prison, which is the prison of the body. And I said, 'He who hears, let him get up from the deep sleep.' And he wept and shed tears. Bitter tears he wiped from himself and he said, 'Who is it that calls my name, and from where has this hope come to me, while I am in the chains of the prison?' And I said, 'I am the Pronoia of the pure light; I am the thinking of the virginal Spirit, who raised you up to the honored place. Arise and remember that it is you who hearkened, and follow your root, which is I, the merciful one, and guard yourself against the angels of poverty and the demons of chaos and all those who ensnare you, and beware of the deep sleep and the enclosure of the inside of Hades."

Frederik Wisse, trans., "Apocryphon of John" in *Early Christian Writings*, accessed November 17, 2020, http://www.earlychristianwritings.com/text/apocryphonjohn.html.

the sin of their ancestor. Doesn't the offspring of Eve include males as well?) But remember from chapter 2, *Eve was not cursed.* Only the serpent and the ground were cursed. What God addressed to Adam and Eve was a description, not a prescription, of how life would change now that they had introduced sin into his creation.

Would God continue to punish all women for the sin of Eve? Timothy was working with a community of believers. They had already put their faith in Jesus Christ. They had been made holy and blameless before God. In his lavish grace, they had been redeemed, their trespasses forgiven (see Eph. 1:4–7). In the previous chapter, Paul had just testified of the mercy and grace of God given to him, "the chief of sinners." To think that God would forgive Paul but continue to make all women accountable for Eve's sin seems very unlikely. It is an attack on the very grace of God (see Rom. 5:19).

God's mercy and forgiveness were bountiful even to those in the Old Testament who were under the law. Yes, he warned the Israelites that "He will by no means leave the guilty unpunished, inflicting the punishment of fathers on the children and on the grandchildren to the third and fourth generations" (Exod. 34:7).[21] This was said to Israel *as a nation* about when they would turn away from God. Hundreds of years later, this came to pass. The people of God, after many years of rebellion, were conquered by Assyria and then Babylon, carried off into captivity as a punishment for their sin.

But the prophet Ezekiel reassured the *individual* exiles in Babylon of God's mercy: "The person who sins will die. A son will not suffer the punishment for the father's guilt, nor will the father suffer the

---

21. Lev. 26:38–39 also warns: "You will perish among the nations, and your enemies' land will consume you. So those of you who may be left will rot away because of their wrongdoing in the lands of your enemies; and also because of the wrongdoing of their forefathers they will rot away with them." But this follows with "If their uncircumcised heart is humbled so that they then make amends for their wrongdoing, then I will remember My covenant with Jacob" in verses 41 and 42. Exod. 34:6–7 characterizes the actions of God: "the LORD, the LORD God, compassionate and merciful, slow to anger, and abounding in faithfulness and truth; who keeps faithfulness for thousands, who forgives wrongdoing, violation of His Law, and sin."

punishment for the son's guilt; the righteousness of the righteous will be upon himself" (Ezek. 18:20). There was a hope even then to escape the punishment for their forefathers' sin: God would deal with them independently. Each person was responsible for themselves.

So in light of what the Old Testament and New Testament teach about God's forgiveness, God's continually holding women accountable for Eve's fall makes little sense.[22]

Reason #3: "But women will be preserved through childbirth—if they continue in faith, love, and sanctity, with moderation."
Part of my seminary education included writing position papers on difficult texts. We were not marked on what interpretive position we took, but rather on how we got there; the goal was to back up a doctrinal position conclusively with a stream of logic from Scripture.

Of the many papers, the most difficult assignment was 1 Timothy 2:15. The whole class struggled. How can someone be saved through childbirth? Paul is very clear in many other places it is not by works we are saved, but through faith. It is God's grace that enables our salvation (see Eph. 2:8–9). Certainly not bearing children!

In the weeks leading up to the due date, we all discussed the possible positions at length over coffee. Some thought Paul was speaking of sanctification, that God would use the challenges of childbirth and raising children to purify women. Some wondered if Paul was giving an alternative to teaching for women: instead of "usurping authority" in the church, they could receive fulfillment through bearing and raising their children. Finally, others were thinking the verse referred to Mary. In childbirth, she bore the Savior of the world, who ultimately provided salvation to all, including herself.

---

22. People who assume that women are gullible neglect the examples in Scripture of women that led with wisdom and skill. Abigail was a wise and prudent woman (1 Sam. 25:32–33) as was Queen Esther, whom God brought to the kingdom "for such a time as this" (Esther 4:14). There were also the resourceful midwives in the story of Moses, who found a way to keep Hebrew babies alive (Exod. 1:17–21), Jael who outwitted General Sisera (Judg. 4:17–22), the Syrophoenician woman who interacted with Jesus in intelligent faith (Matt. 15:21–28), and Deborah the judge (Judg. 4–5).

Every day before class, we tried to settle on what made the most sense. We frequently switched our respective positions as we debated academic journal articles and pertinent Scripture. Finally, the paper was due. I printed out what I had, still not happy with where I had tentatively landed on the issue, and headed to class.

As I handed in my assignment, I told the professor, "I feel like I should qualify this paper with a statement on the title page: 'As of 10 a.m. this morning, this is Julie Coleman's position. It is subject to change, because maybe even tomorrow she will believe differently.'" He laughed, because he knew just how challenging this verse was.

Now, these many years later, flipping the verse around to the negative has moved me in a new direction. Was there someone claiming that women could *not* be saved while she labored as a mother? Was Paul for a third time reacting to a bad teaching?

The Gnostics taught that the requirements for salvation included releasing the spirit (or divine spark) from the evil soul so it could return to be united with the highest deity. Childbearing made that task almost impossible, because the divine spark was scattered into one's offspring, trapping it in their evil souls.[23] There is historical record of a pagan priest who renounced all fleshly procreation.[24] A later group, the Phibionites (who inherited the Nicolaitan traditions) rejected marriage and were violently opposed to childbirth.[25] Saint Epiphanius wrote that when a person (soul) "turns out to have

---

23. Kroeger and Kroeger, *I Suffer Not a Woman*, 174. For example, in *The Gospel According to the Egyptians*, Jesus is quoted as saying, "I came to destroy the works of the female." Salome asks: "Until when shall men die?" and Jesus tells her, "As long as women bear children." Salome answers, "I would have done better had I never given birth to a child." Clement of Alexandria, *Stromata* 3/5, 63–6 (John-Paul Migne, Patrologia Graeca [PG] 8.1;1193.) Also available at http://www.earlychristianwritings.com.

24. Hippolytus, *Refutation of All Heresies* 5.8.19 (Migne, PG 16.3.3146). Hippolytus wrote: "do not you plainly preach to your pupils . . . you forbid marriage, the procreation of children, [and] the abstaining from meat which God has created."

25. Epiphanius, *Panarion* 26.13, 2–3 (Migne, PG 41.352–53).

fathered a son, it is detained below [on earth] until it can take its own children up and restore them to itself."[26]

It is likely Paul is refuting this erroneous doctrine. He is assuring women that procreation and childbearing will not be a hindrance to their salvation. They should just continue to live their lives with trust in the Lord and his Word.

All three reasons Paul gives for prohibiting a certain woman to teach seem to be related to first-century heresy. We will now turn back to the statement in verse 12 itself with this context in mind.

Was Paul Stating a Universal Prohibition on Teaching to All Women in Every Age and Place?

Paul is likely speaking about an individual who is mixing her new-found Christianity with the pagan teaching from which she came, corrupting the very gospel of Christ.

There is a somewhat similar situation in Acts 18. A man from Alexandria, named Apollos, was an eloquent and bold preacher. This man knew his Scriptures and fervently taught them in the synagogues. But there was a gaping hole in his background: his understanding was limited to what was available while John the Baptist preached in the wilderness. Luke tells us that when Priscilla and Aquila heard him, easily detecting what Apollos was missing, they took him aside and filled him in on the rest of the Messiah's story (see Acts 18:24–28).

Apollos had things to learn before he could resume teaching. That remedy seems comparable to what Paul instructs here: "A woman must quietly receive instruction with entire submissiveness" (1 Tim. 2:11). The woman needed correction. She needed to spend some time getting her theology straight, separating her past beliefs from the true Word of God. She should not be allowed to teach until she understood. That understanding would only come if she had an attitude

---

26. Epiphanius, *Panarion* 26.13, 2–3 (Migne, PG 41.352–53).

of humility and receptiveness to the whole truth. She must submit herself to those who could foster that understanding.[27]

Her present attitude was not commendable. One important key to understanding Paul's description of her teaching is the word translated as "usurp authority," the Greek *authenteo*. As stated earlier, this verb occurs only once in the New Testament and only two other times in contemporary secular writing. So there is little context available to discern what it meant at the time of Paul.

The earliest usages (found in earlier extrabiblical writing) meant "to be responsible for something, usually murder."[28] When used in the previous century, it was not a positive word. It referred to one who killed with his own hand. In the second century, it was used for someone who acted on their own authority, exercising harmful power over another.[29] It is also found in an Egyptian legal document, describing someone who claimed property for his own, wrongly usurping something that others had a right to share.[30] By the second century, *authenteo* conveyed a sense of having power or authority. It implied dominance, wielding power and authority over the weaker.[31]

In the body of Christ, no one was to dominate. Paul told the Ephesians to all be subject to one another in the fear of Christ (see Eph. 5:21). He wrote the Corinthians that no one person was to be considered above the rest; all were members of the same body, all significant

---

27. This is also comparable to what Paul says about women in 1 Cor. 14:34–35, with the same connection of *silence* and *learning*: "The women are to keep silent in the churches. . . . If they desire to learn anything, let them ask their own husbands." Silence and submission was a formula used in the ancient Near East and indicated not only a readiness to hear the will of God, but to obey it; Kroeger and Kroeger, *I Suffer Not a Woman*, 32.
28. Kroeger and Kroeger, *I Suffer Not a Woman*, 85.
29. Thayer, as described on BlueLetterBible.org. BDAG defines its use in 1 Timothy as assuming a stance of independent authority, give orders to, or dictate to (BDAG, *authentin*, 264).
30. The Krogers point out that *teaching* and *authenteo* are linked together by *oude*, so it could be possible Paul meant them as one entity. Together they might convey one idea: *authentin* explains what sort, or what manner of teachings are being prohibited (Kroeger and Kroeger, *I Suffer Not a Woman*, 88–89).
31. Kroeger and Kroeger, *I Suffer Not a Woman*, 91.

in their person and service, all under one head: Jesus Christ (see 1 Cor. 12:4–26). If one woman was domineering over anyone, she was out of line. In addition, her teaching held some shocking elements, tenets from pagan cults disguised as teaching from Scripture. In light of what is contained in 1 Timothy 2, there is just not enough evidence to be confident that Paul was laying out a universal restriction on women teaching rather than addressing a specific problem in Ephesus.

One last note: Paul lays out church leadership credentials for elders and deacons in 1 Timothy 3:1–13. Some assume these are for males only, which would lend support to restricting women from teaching (which is also a leadership role). But while a typical translation begins "if any *man* aspires to the office of overseer, it is a fine work *he* desires to do," the Greek pronouns throughout these verses are actually not male, but gender-neutral. A better translation would be, "whoever aspires to the office of overseer, it is a fine work they desire to do." No gender is indicated.

In that section, Paul also uses the phrase "the husband of one wife." In the culture at the time, this idiom was not only applied to males, but was also used on epitaphs to describe women faithful to their husbands. Doctor Instone Brewer states, "In New Testament time those phrases meant 'a one-woman man' or a 'one-man woman', i.e., someone who was faithful."[32]

Many view 1 Timothy 2:11–16 as the lens through which we should view every other New Testament text about women. In light of what we have seen, it would seem to be a far better idea to turn the telescope around and view 1 Timothy 2 through the lens of the other New Testament texts.

- In 1 Corinthians 11:2–16, women were prophesying (which involves instruction from the words of God) during church gatherings.

---

32. The latter is found later, in 1 Timothy 5:9. Ann Maxwell-Nithsdale Nyland, *The Source New Testament: With Extensive Notes on Greek Word Meaning* (Australia: Smith and Stirling Publishing, 2007), 413.

- In Acts 18:26, Priscilla is positively portrayed teaching a man (a respected preacher!).
- In Luke 10:38–42, Mary sits at the feet of Jesus, when it was a cultural assumption that this interaction was only for men.
- In Romans 16:1 and 16:7, Paul greets Phoebe as a deacon and Junia as an apostle.
- In John 20:17, Jesus sent women to proclaim the resurrection to the male disciples.
- Paul calls women "fellow workers" in Philippians 4:2–3 and in Romans 16:3.
- Paul gives no limitations on gender when listing spiritual gifts in Romans, 1 Corinthians, or Ephesians. He only says the Holy Spirit decides who is given what, not us, and that each one should be using their gift for the common good.
- In Galatians 3:26–28, Paul wrote the Galatians that all dividing lines had been erased between formerly contentious factions.

Paul did not mention restricting a female from teaching in any other of his letters. He was respectful and enthusiastic about what women contributed to the church. Rather than being dismissive of women, he wrote of the mutual respect men and women needed to cultivate and the need we have for each other.

Good News for Today

As we have worked through the biblical texts (so far) related to women and their roles among God's people in the Old Testament and in his church in the New Testament, we have seen that women were not only allowed to participate in ministry and leadership, but were *encouraged* to do so. Paul knew the importance of every member in the body using their gifts to build up the church. The health of the church body is greatly enhanced by women's unique contributions to ministry.

I have seen how a woman's voice could be instrumental in effecting positive change within the church. A friend of mine lived in an abusive marriage for many years. Over time, she had approached leadership in churches for support, but her husband made no changes in his addictive, abusive behavior. She was always given the same answer from the male leaders: forgive him and continue to submit to his authority.

The situation grew increasingly violent. She finally accepted the sad reality: she could not trust the church to do the right thing by her and her children. Finally, after one particularly violent night involving her children, she filed for a divorce. Not long after, the elders asked to meet with her again. She agreed to do so, but with one caveat: the leaders' wives must be in attendance at that meeting.

She came to the group well prepared. She handed out a meeting agenda and some important Bible study notes she had made before filing for divorce. Bolstered by the presence of the wives in the room, she boldly shared the embarrassing, intimate details of life with a husband addicted to pornography with a propensity for violent rage.

The whole tenor of the meeting was different than the previous meetings she'd had with the elders. The husbands seemed to find a new perspective while hearing her story with their wives sitting next to them. Suddenly, their pat answers and stern advice that she should keep going back into the situation was seen for the foolishness it had been.

Three days later, she received an email from the church leadership. It was unlike anything she'd previously received from them. Expressing their new understanding of her situation, they promised to stand by her and her children as she went through the painful process of ending her marriage.

The change of attitude went beyond her situation. Other women in that church who had been living with abuse were then able to approach leadership without fear. The pastor formed a new committee and asked my friend to be on it, and to find ways to support women who had previously or were presently suffering under an abuser.

I was so thankful to hear that her church finally began to see the painful reality of some people in their pews on Sunday morning. God used the story of one woman and the support of other females to open their eyes and bring a new understanding which might never have been reached without that female perspective.

One of my seminary professors has a ministry for churches that have gone through a rough patch or a church split. His first step is to get as much information as possible from those on the inside track—specifically, the elders of that body. But when they meet for that purpose, he requires their wives to be in attendance as well. He knows an all-male board can miss certain aspects in any situation. Women have a keen awareness of what is happening in the body. They offer a perspective that, combined with their husbands', gives a much more balanced idea of what in the church needs addressing. We need each other.

There is the same kind of benefit in being taught from a woman's perspective. Equality does not equal uniformity. We each have something to bring to the table. But there is great variety in what we bring. The teaching team at my church has four members: two men and two women. We each do one-fourth of the Sunday sermons. All of us are gifted speakers and dedicated to accurately teaching the Word of God. But the similarities end there. We have four very different personalities and teaching styles, four different points of view, and four different sets of strengths and weaknesses. I recently joked with my husband that together, the four of us make the perfect preacher. It's never boring on a Sunday morning, that's for sure! There is a great deal to be gained by allowing every person to be used by God in however he has gifted them. It benefits the entire body. We are missing out on so much when only the men are allowed to teach.

Diversity is a manifestation of the endless creativity of God. Males and females each have their strengths. When we work together, as teammates and colleagues, we are better than we are without each other. It's time to reevaluate. It's time to give women the freedom they need to serve Christ without limits. And, in part, that means giving women the freedom to teach. Doing so will transform us all.

Chapter 9

Does God Expect Husbands to Be in Charge of Their Wives?

And do not get drunk with wine, in which there is debauchery, but be filled with the Spirit, speaking to one another in psalms and hymns and spiritual songs, singing and making melody with your hearts to the Lord; always giving thanks for all things in the name of our Lord Jesus Christ to our God and Father; and subject yourselves to one another in the fear of Christ.

Wives, subject yourselves to your own husbands, as to the Lord. For the husband is the head of the wife, as Christ also is the head of the church, He Himself being the Savior of the body. But as the church is subject to Christ, so also the wives ought to be to their husbands in everything.

Husbands, love your wives, just as Christ also loved the church and gave Himself up for her, so that He might sanctify her, having cleansed her by the washing of water with the word, that He might present to Himself the church in all her glory, having no spot or wrinkle or any such thing; but that she would be holy and blameless. So husbands also ought to love their own wives as their own bodies. He who loves his own wife loves himself; for no one ever hated his own flesh, but nourishes and cherishes it, just as Christ also does the church, because we are parts of His body. For this reason a man shall leave his father and his mother and be joined to his wife, and the two shall become one flesh. This mystery is great; but I am speaking with

reference to Christ and the church. Nevertheless, as for you individually, each husband is to love his own wife the same as himself, and
the wife must see to it that she respects her husband.

—Ephesians 5:18–33

Focus on Ephesians 5

John was raised in a Christian home, but his biggest spiritual influence was his grandmother. She often talked with him about God and how loving him meant obedience to his Word. She practiced what she preached; through the years he watched her live out her obedience by submitting to his grandfather . . . and his abuse. Just like she thought the Word of God said.

He fell in love and married a woman who believed in Jesus, but when he became involved in a church, she hung back. Church leaders felt this was unacceptable and hounded him to "get his wife in line." He told me: "That's when I started fighting with my wife. They even convinced me that my wife had demons (specifically, Jezebel), and that she needed deliverance. I was dumb enough to believe them and even dumber enough to actually tell her that during a heated argument. My marriage almost ended. Our home became so explosive that I had no choice but to back off and reevaluate my views. I realized that if this [model of marriage] truly was God's design and intention for us, it shouldn't be accompanied by so much friction."

Is this what it means to be a living example of Ephesians 5? Does this passage dictate a hierarchy in marriage? Is it the husband's role to rule the household and to keep his wife in line, as those church leaders believed? Ephesians 5:21–33, at a superficial read, could lead people into thinking exactly that. But a closer look reveals a different story—something very different than what was modeled for John while growing up.

Paul was purposeful in his letter writing. He frequently wrote to address a specific church issue, as we have already seen in both 1 Corinthians and 1 Timothy. The same is true for his letter to the Ephesians. But what was his purpose in writing to the Ephesians?

The church at Ephesus was planted by Paul (with help from Priscilla and Aquila) during Paul's second missionary journey (see Acts 18:18–21). It was located in what is now western Turkey, near the coast on the Asia Minor peninsula. The population of 300,000 was mostly Gentile, but Palestinian Jews had been a part of the community since 5 BC.[1] The church in Ephesus was comprised of both Gentiles and Jews.

There was a divide between these two groups. To address this, Paul opened his letter with all of the things believing Jews and Gentiles had in common:

- God had made them holy and blameless and had adopted every one of them into his family.
- Each had been redeemed, forgiven, and now shared an inheritance with Christ.
- All believers had the Holy Spirit permanently indwelling them, which, among other things, served as a seal guaranteeing their future inheritance.
- All had been saved through the grace of God.

Paul also knew the division between the two groups ran deep, in part because Judaism had institutionalized a hierarchy between the races. In the temple, there were boundaries designated by knee-high walls for the factions of worshipers. The outmost court, which ran around the outside perimeter of the temple, was the only place Gentiles could enter.[2] The inner courts, for women, then men, were for Jews only.

---

1. At the end of the third century BC, Antiochus transferred 5,000 Jews from Babylonia and Mesopotamia to key places in the general area of Ephesus. Ronald F. Youngblood, ed., *Nelson's New Illustrated Bible Dictionary*, (Nashville: Thomas Nelson, 1995), 406–7.
2. In fact, in intervals on that wall warnings were posted. One such sign was found in 1871, which reads: "No foreigner is to go beyond the balustrade and the plaza of the temple zone. Whoever is caught doing so will have himself to blame." Bible History, "Temple Warning Inscription," accessed November 12, 2021, https://www.bible-history.com/archaeology/israel/temple-warning.html.

But Jesus eliminated what stood between them when he died for all humankind. "For He Himself is our peace, who made both groups into one and broke down the barrier of the dividing wall, by abolishing in His flesh the hostility . . . so that in Himself He might make the two one new person, in this way establishing peace; and that He might reconcile them both in one body to God through the cross, by it having put to death the hostility" (Eph. 2:14–16). The human institutions upholding barriers between races were now obliterated; Jesus died to eradicate that divide. So, Paul continued, "You are no longer strangers and foreigners, but you are fellow citizens with the saints, and are of God's household" (2:19).

Much of the rest of his letter is practical in nature, in which Paul gives ways to live out that truth as one fellowship.

- "Walk in a manner worthy of the calling with which you have been called, with all humility and gentleness, with patience, bearing with one another in love,
- being diligent to keep the unity of the Spirit in the bond of peace.
- There is one body and one Spirit . . . one Lord, one faith, one baptism, one God and Father of all who is over all and through all and in all" (Eph. 4:1–6).

What Is the Context of Ephesians 5:22–33?

Paul begins the section with "Do not get drunk with wine . . . but be filled with the Spirit" (v. 18). Since we already have the Spirit living in us, what does Paul mean by "be filled"? He is talking about letting the Spirit have his impact on us, fully living "under the influence," using the metaphor of alcohol-induced behavior to explain the nature of yieldedness.[3]

---

3. The word "filled" (*plēroō*) carries the sense of "fulfill, be complete" (BDAG, *plēroō*, 827–28). While we are already indwelled, we can grieve the Spirit when we do not align ourselves with his guidance and purpose: "Do not grieve the Holy Spirit of God, by whom you were sealed for the day of redemption" (Eph. 4:30). To be filled with the Spirit is to allow him to guide our actions and our hearts.

Paul then gives four ways that "being filled" will look fleshed out in believers. Each way Paul gives is a participial phrase (a phrase beginning with an *-ing* verb), making the list easy to spot in the Greek. Unfortunately, this is not so obvious in some English translations. Each participial verb phrase modifies the imperative *be filled*. Paul's grammatical structure in verses 18–21 looks like this:

Be filled with the Spirit—

- *Speaking* to one another in psalms and hymns and spiritual songs
- *Singing and making melody* with your heart to the Lord
- *Giving thanks* always for all things in the name of our Lord Jesus . . .
- *Submitting* to one another in the fear of Christ.[4]

Paul then gives examples of submitting one to another, both within the context of marriage. Note that the word *submit* is not even in verse 22 (in the original Greek):[5]

Wives, to husbands
Husbands, love your wives

What Does It Mean to Submit?

There are many different possible meanings attributed to this Greek word translated "submit," *hypotasso*. Therefore, the context is very important. Some think it simply means to obey. There are two reasons

---

4. While two of the major modern versions (NASB/NIV) translate *hypotasso* (as subject/submit) in v. 21 as an imperative, the original Greek verb is a participle, as reflected in three of the major modern versions (CSB/ESV/NKJV). As a participle, it more appropriately functions as detailing the command to "be filled" in v. 18.
5. The verb is not in v. 22 in most Greek texts. Most translations put v. 22 into a new section after v. 21, when v. 22 clearly depends on the verb in v. 21 (and these translations add another verb to v. 22). The result is that many teachers begin teaching on wives and husbands with v. 22: "Wives, submit to husbands," ignoring the fact that Paul has just told them that every believer is to submit to each other.

we find in the text that do not support that definition. First, Paul is telling the whole Ephesian church to submit to each other.[6] How can everyone obey everyone else? Second, Paul uses a different word when writing: "Children, obey your parents in the Lord, for this is right" (Eph. 6:1). The verb Paul uses here is not *hypotasso*, but *hypakouo*, a completely different word. If Paul was instructing both wives and children to obey, why wouldn't he have used the same verb for both?

My husband, while speaking about submission, once called a young boy up to the stage and sat him on a tall stool. After asking him about his age and grade, he looked at the audience and said, "Whatever submit means, it is something I need to do for this kindergartener, and he needs to do for me." The point of the illustration? Every believer is not to obey every other believer, but we are to submit to every other believer in the fear of Christ.

So, if Paul does not mean for wives to obey, what is he asking them to do? Originally, *hypotasso* was a term that stressed a relationship to superiors. But, according to the *Theological Dictionary of the New Testament*, the verb does not immediately carry the thought of obedience in the New Testament.[7] Rather, it suggested "that the general rule demands readiness to renounce one's own will for the sake of others, . . . and to give precedence to others."[8]

This is readily seen in what Paul wrote to another church, in Philippi, while describing the necessary mindset of believers: "Make my joy complete by being of the same mind, maintaining the same love, united in spirit, intent on one purpose. Do nothing from selfishness or empty conceit, but with humility *consider one another as more important than yourselves; do not merely look out for your own personal interests, but also for the interests of others*" (Phil. 2:2–4, emphasis mine).

Here in Ephesians, Paul gives the imperative to submit to each

---

6. Paul uses the pronoun *allelous* (which is plural) in Eph. 4:2, 25, and 32.
7. Gerhard Kittel and Gerhard Friedrich, eds., Geoffrey W. Bromiley, trans., *Theological Dictionary of the New Testament*, vol. 8 (Grand Rapids: Eerdmans, 1972), 41 (hereafter cited as *TDNT*).
8. Kittel and Friedrich, *TDNT*, 45.

other "in the fear of Christ" (5:21). Why would Paul put our relationship with Jesus and fear in the same sentence?

At a Communion service I attended years ago, one young believer stood and recounted a narrow miss he had experienced the evening before. He'd lost control of his car on a patch of ice, and as he spun around, for a few heart-stopping moments he saw the quickly approaching headlights of an oncoming car. Somehow, at the last second, that car managed to steer around him.

When his car came to a stop, he pulled off the road and sat shaking. He thought about what could have been; he could be dead. He could have killed the occupants of that second car. God had just saved him from a terrible thing. He told his fellowship, "All I could think was, 'Whew! What it could have been!'"

His voice choked as he added, "Later, I thought of what else could have been in my life: the awful eternal fate I could have had because of my sin. But Jesus swooped down and saved me from that terrible thing. And with an even more grateful heart, I again thought, 'Whew! What it could have been!'" I believe that's the kind of fear Paul was talking about.

Peter puts it this way: "Conduct yourselves in fear during the time of your stay on earth; knowing that you were not redeemed with perishable things like silver or gold from your futile way of life inherited from your forefathers, but with precious blood" (1 Peter 1:17–19). Our fear is that we not step on the grace of God by living by our own agenda, but to respond to what we have been given through Christ as people who have been redeemed.

Jesus has accomplished all the things that enabled our salvation. We all stand on equal ground at the cross; there was nothing any of us could do but believe. Therefore, our only "head" is Christ, for he paid the price for our redemption. Salvation was given to us by the grace (undeserved merit) of God. In light of that reality, every believer should submit to the other in a spirit of mutual humility.[9] Humility that comes from fearfully understanding what we really deserved.

---

9. I. Howard Marshall, "Mutual Love and Submission in Marriage," *Discovering*

What Does Paul Mean Concerning Husbands and Wives?

Example #1: Wives, to husbands . . .
The first example Paul gives to flesh out his submission imperative centers on the wife in a marriage. The verb is implied from the verse before ("submitting to one another"). Paul gives the reason for this submission: "For the husband is the head of the wife, as Christ also is the head of the church, He Himself being the Savior of the body" (Eph. 5:23).

How is Jesus our *head*?

We actually don't have to use conjecture on that; Paul qualifies Christ's role as *head* with his next phrase: "He Himself being the Savior of the body." To be our Savior, Jesus put aside his own needs for the good of humankind. Though blameless, he suffered for the sin of the world. He gave his life so that we could live. There's no sense of authority here. Paul is defining headship in terms of self-sacrifice.

If you will remember from chapter 6, there are two Greek words that can be translated as *head*: *arche* (emphasizing authority) and *kephale*. In this verse, Paul chooses *kephale*. The vast majority of times this word occurs in the Septuagint, it designated either the literal part of a body on top of the neck or a point of origination.[10] Jesus was the source of our salvation.

Before we can interpret this first example, we need to look at the second one.

Biblical Equality: Complementarity Without Hierarchy, ed. Ronald W. Pierce, Rebecca Merrill Groothuis, and Gordon D. Fee (Downers Grove, IL: IVP Academic, 2005), 197.

10. In the Septuagint, a Greek translation of the Old Testament, *kephale* is used like this in 165 out of 171 occurrences. Philip Payne, *Man and Woman, One in Christ: An Exegetical and Theological Study of Paul's Letters* (Grand Rapids: Zondervan, 2009), 119. By far the majority of occurrences of *kephale* mean the literal part of the body. (In the Septuagint, six of those occurrences translate *rosh*—which designated a leader—as *kephale*. The other 160-odd times a different word is used.)

Example #2: Husbands, love your wives . . .

In verse 25, Paul now turns his attention to the men: "Husbands, love your wives." Again, he uses the example of Jesus to clarify mutual submission: ". . . just as Christ also loved the church and gave Himself up for her." Paul goes on to describe the purposes of Christ's love: "so that He might sanctify her, having cleansed her by the washing of water with the word, that He might present to Himself the church in all her glory . . . that she would be holy and blameless" (Eph. 5:26–27).

Paul defines love in his first letter to the Corinthians: "Love is patient, love is kind, it is not jealous; love does not brag, it is not arrogant. It does not act disgracefully, it does not seek its own benefit; it is not provoked, does not keep an account a wrong suffered, it does not rejoice in unrighteousness, but rejoices with the truth; it keeps every confidence, it believes all things, hopes all things, endures all things" (1 Cor. 13:4–7).

Not seeking its own benefit. Not keeping an account of a wrong suffered. Humility. Self-sacrifice. Sounds a lot like submission, right? Paul's examples of wives and husbands are two sides of the same submission coin. They fit beautifully within the context of the mutual submission Paul is asking of the church. Gilbert Bilezikian observes, "Whenever Christ is upheld as the model for husbands to follow, it is not his power, his lordship, and his authority that are presented as the traits to emulate, but his humility, his abnegation [self-denial], and his servant behavior."[11]

Like Jesus did for the church, the husband is to lay down his life for his wife. Paul says that Jesus's sacrifice was to sanctify the body. Sanctification is the process of being set apart.[12] Paul was not focusing on the immediate work of regeneration (when new life is given). Sanctification is a work God continues within us long after salvation,

---

11. Gilbert Bilezikian, *Beyond Sex Roles*, 3rd ed. (Grand Rapids: Baker Academic, 2006), 128.

12. BDAG, *agiazo*, 9–10.

slowly transforming us into the image of Christ (see Phil. 1:6; Rom. 8:29).

As the *kephale*, Jesus "determines not merely the being of the body, but also the fulfilment of its life."[13] The husband is to do the same for his wife, giving precedence to her spiritual growth. "Love is explicitly defined in this passage in terms of self-sacrificial service, not in terms of his authority."[14] He is to love his wife as he loves his own body. He is to nourish and cherish her. Paul uses the word *nourish*, which means to provide food, as a metaphor for spiritual nourishment.[15] The husband is to selflessly give his wife tender, loving care, all the while enabling her to reach her full potential in Christ. After all, Paul reasons, it is the way God designed a marriage relationship to operate: that the two will be one flesh, truly unified in their mutual desire to enable the other to fulfill their God-given potential.

There is not a hint of hierarchy in any of this.

You may have noticed that Paul gives much more space to the example of the husband's submission than he does of the wife's. In antiquity, the traditional role for women was to be supportive and sub-servient. In ancient writings, Roman women were portrayed as "meek, quiet, . . . 'shy', and 'self-conscious' in the presence of men."[16] When Paul states that wives should submit, it would not have seemed radical to the letter's recipients. It was the expected behavior of the times.

But for the husbands, Paul's imperative to love their wives was something quite different than their culturally defined role. (In other ancient literature, the responsibility of the husband to love his wife was not explicitly stressed as much as the wife was told to submit.[17]) So Paul took time to get very specific, grounding his explanation in the example of Jesus.

---

13. Kittel and Friedrich, *TDNT*, vol. 3, 680.
14. Craig S. Keener, *Paul, Women, and Wives: Marriage and Women's Ministry in the Letters of Paul* (Grand Rapids: Baker Academic, 1992), 169.
15. BDAG, *ektrepho*, 311.
16. Keener, *Paul*, 167.
17. Keener, *Paul*, 167.

Both husband and wife are to submit, because the whole church is to live in submission to each other. They can do so through dependence on the Spirit, who is at work in them, providing the strength and power to put themselves aside. Paul began Ephesians 5: "Therefore be imitators of God, as beloved children; and walk in love, just as Christ also loved you and gave Himself up for us, an offering and a sacrifice to God as a fragrant aroma" (Eph. 5:1–2).

Paul is clearly leading the Ephesians "out of patriarchalism into a different kind of relationship that mirrors more adequately the mutual love and respect that is God's purpose for his redeemed people."[18] Mutual submission would abolish all boundary lines between Jew and Greek, master and slave, and husband and wife.

In another letter, written at the same time to the church at Colossae, Paul again urges unity that is possible after a second birth: "hav[ing] put on the new self, which is being renewed to a true knowledge according to the image of the One who created him—a renewal in which there is no distinction between Greek and Jew, circumcised and uncircumcised, barbarian, Scythian, slave, and free, but Christ is all, and in all" (Col. 3:10–11).

The text of Colossians 3 is strikingly similar as Paul advises how the church should interact with each other. His instructions are bookmarked by two statements, urging them "whatever you do in word or deed, do everything in the name of the Lord Jesus" in verse 17 and later restates this in verse 23: "as for the Lord and not for people." Submitting to each other is in reality submitting to God's will for his church.

Good News for Today

A friend of mine recently arrived at church one Sunday morning and greeted a man whose wife was friendly with her daughter. She asked him where his spouse was and was taken aback by his answer. He explained that his wife had purchased groceries that he felt to be superfluous to their needs. "She is a bit put out with me," he told

---

18. Marshall, "Mutual Love and Submission," *Discovering Biblical Equality*, 204.

her. "She wanted to come to church, but I told her she needed to stay home and think about what she had done."

I'm quite sure that Paul would not have approved of this man wielding power over his wife. Interestingly, the only time that the word *authority*[19] was used by Paul in the context of marriage was in 1 Corinthians 7: "The wife does not have authority over her own body, but the husband does; and likewise the husband also does not have authority over his own body, but the wife does" (v. 4). If in the most intimate part of the marriage relationship, the lack of authority over the other is mutual, we can assume that mutuality should pervade the rest of the marriage.

This is very good news for today. When husband and wife work together, each valued, respected, and appreciated, the marriage is better for it. Remember my friend at the beginning of this chapter, who was told to "get his wife in line"? After researching the Scripture for himself, John was brought to a new understanding by the Lord. He no longer felt it was his responsibility to be in charge of his wife. They began to practice mutual respect and self-sacrificing love for each other. Their relationship quickly turned into something much healthier and more reflective of the Savior they followed.

He told me: "Now we actually take turns leading. She leads on some aspects of our lives, and I lead at the others, according to our strengths. We make the big decisions together, like the decision to uproot our family and move last summer. But I think the biggest change is the one within myself. It's that part where I look at her as an equal. She is my equal. I know it within my innermost being.

"Now I pity those men who remain encumbered with a hierarchical marriage view. If they would just step back and let their wives come into their own, instead of suppressing and controlling them, they would find their lives are so much more blessed."

An understanding of the truth always brings freedom. The mutual submission that Paul commands in Ephesians 5 is God's way to the healthiest of marriages.

---

19. Greek: *exousia*.

Chapter 10

What Is the Scriptural Definition of a Godly Woman?

Keep your behavior excellent among the Gentiles, so that in the thing in which they slander you as evildoers, they may because of your good deeds, as they observe them, glorify God on the day of visitation.

Submit yourselves for the Lord's sake to every human institution, whether to a king as the one in authority, or to governors as sent by him for the punishment of evildoers and the praise of those who do right. For such is the will of God, that by doing right you silence the ignorance of foolish people. Act as free people, and do not use your freedom as a covering for evil, but use it as bond-servants of God. Honor all people, love the brotherhood, fear God, honor the king.

Servants, be subject to your masters with all respect, not only to those who are good and gentle, but also to those who are harsh. For this finds favor, if for the sake of conscience toward God a person endures grief when suffering unjustly. For what credit is there if, when you sin and are harshly treated, you endure it with patience? But if when you do what is right and suffer for it you patiently endure it, this finds favor with God.

For you have been called for this purpose, because Christ also suffered for you, leaving you an example, so that you would follow in His steps, He who committed no sin, nor was any deceit found in His mouth; and while being abusively insulted, He did not insult in return; while suffering, He did not threaten, but kept entrusting

Himself to Him who judges righteously; and He Himself brought our sins in His body up on the cross, so that we might die to sin and live for righteousness; by His wounds you were healed. For you were continually straying like sheep, but now you have returned to the Shepherd and Guardian of your souls.

In the same way, you wives, be subject to your own husbands so that even if any of them are disobedient to the word, they may be won over without a word by the behavior of their wives, as they observe your pure and respectful behavior. Your adornment must not be merely the external—braiding the hair, wearing gold jewelry, or putting on apparel; but it should be the hidden person of the heart, with the imperishable quality of a gentle and quiet spirit, which is precious in the sight of God. For in this way the holy women of former times, who hoped in God, also used to adorn themselves, being subject to their own husbands, just as Sarah obeyed Abraham, calling him lord; and you have proved to be her children if you do what is right without being frightened by any fear.

You husbands in the same way, live with your wives in an understanding way, as with someone weaker, since she is a woman; and show her honor as a fellow heir of the grace of life, so that your prayers will not be hindered.

To sum up, all of you be harmonious, sympathetic, loving, compassionate, and humble; not returning evil for evil or insult for insult, but giving a blessing instead; for you were called for the very purpose that you would inherit a blessing.

—1 Peter 2:12–3:9

Focus on 1 Peter 3

When I was young and still single, a man from our young adults' group and I were on our way to visit mutual friends. I almost had declined the offer to come—this guy was not one of my favorite people. He'd been making the rounds, dating every young woman in the church in search of a wife. Before getting in the car, I'd told my dad of my misgivings about sharing a two-hour car ride with him.

My dad asked why I felt the guy was so hard to take. I told him, "First of all, he's preachy. And he doesn't respect women on any spiritual level. He thinks all we have to offer is submission."

Dad responded, "You should tell him. You might be doing him a favor." I shook my head. I definitely did not want to get into that kind of interaction. The guy wouldn't hear me, anyway.

But we weren't five minutes along in our trip, when he turned to me and said, "Julie, sometimes I get the feeling you don't like me. Can you tell me why?" Oh, brother. So much for my resolution not to get involved.

I decided he deserved the truth from me. So as kindly as I could, I voiced my concerns over his attitude about women. I didn't want to hurt him. But there was a log the size of a redwood tree in his eye. He needed to start valuing women for who they were in Christ. To my surprise, he listened attentively and even asked a few questions. Finally, he told me in amazement, "Julie, you are the first woman I have ever met that I know for sure I will not marry."

I burst out laughing. "It's good we got that cleared up," I told him. "Because I don't want to marry you, either!"

As ridiculous as his declaration was, it did prick my heart. God had given me a propensity to lead. It came out in positive ways, like when serving as a camp counselor or becoming a schoolteacher. But it also had a negative side—I frequently found myself to be the opposite of the quiet, demure woman that supposedly was Scripture's ideal. Which meant whoever *was* brave enough to marry me might have a tough time surviving my strong personality.

The passage that worried me most was 1 Peter 3: "Wives, be subject to your own husbands, so that . . . they may be won over without a word by the behavior of their wives, as they observe your pure and respectful behavior . . . with the imperishable quality of a gentle and quiet spirit, which is precious in the sight of God" (vv. 1–2, 4).

First Peter 3 contains the lengthiest instruction for wives in the New Testament. At a superficial read, it did not bode well for Julie Zine. Being so headstrong and opinionated, I was pretty sure I was doomed to break the mold.

But is that what Peter meant? That the good women were the ones who kept their mouths shut and bowed to their husbands' authority? That a big personality like mine would never pass muster?

Before we can interpret Peter's instruction, we have some investigative work to do. As always, we must consider the context of the letter as well as the historical situation when Peter wrote.

But yet another challenge in the interpretation of a passage is in identifying the principle at its heart: the universal truth that can be applied in any culture or time period.

Identifying the central idea is key to our understanding of 1 Peter 3. The verses under consideration are only part of a larger section that starts at 2:12 and ends at 3:16. The structure of the passage is easily discernable, since it begins and ends with very similar language (which I like to think of as bookends).

> "Keep your behavior excellent among the Gentiles, so that in the thing in which they slander you as evildoers, they may because of your good deeds . . . glorify God" (2:12).

Submit to government authorities (2:13–17).

Slaves, be submissive to your masters like Jesus was (2:18–25).

Wives, be submissive to your husbands (3:1–6); Husbands, honor your wives (3:7).

"Keep a good conscience, so that in the thing in which you are slandered, those who disparage your good behavior in Christ will be put to shame" (3:16).

What type of "excellent behavior" did Peter ask of his readers? He uses the same word over and over: submission (*hypotasso*).

- He first asks everyone to *submit* themselves for the Lord's sake to every human institution of government.
- He then tells servants to *be submissive* not only to good masters, but also to those who are unreasonable.
- He urges wives to be *submissive* to their unbelieving husbands.
- Finally, he asks husbands to *honor* their wives.[1]

While we might at first be tempted to think that Peter's point is all about submission, I think those bookends are better indicators of his central idea. Peter uses phrases in the beginning and at the end that are close in meaning. Repetition in Scripture is an indicator of emphasis.

Peter's central point was that his readers should be purposeful in how they lived, knowing their actions would communicate the content of their faith to the unbelieving world. He was asking them to keep from muddying the waters to allow an unimpeded view of Christ in us.

---

1. While the word *submission* is not specifically mentioned, we saw in Ephesians 5 that love and honor were expressions of mutual submission between husbands and wives. See chapter 9, pages 158–161.

1 Peter 2:12	1 Peter 3:16
Keep your behavior excellent	Keep a good conscience
In the thing in which they slander you	In the thing in which you are slandered
[That] they may because of your good deeds . . . glorify God	[That] those who disparage your good behavior in Christ will be put to shame

I've seen firsthand how this principle could play out in someone's life. Years ago, a young family came to visit our church, invited by a friend. Chip, the husband, was a bit gruff and awkward, and seated himself up against a side wall where he could stay out of the middle of things. To my surprise, the couple returned the following Sunday. Another family invited them for dinner, and during the meal, explained the gospel of Jesus Christ. The couple received it with open hearts and believed.

The following Sunday, they were back again. But this time, no wall seating for Chip. He and his family settled into the center of the auditorium. Chip was all in from the moment the music started. He sang at the top of his lungs, arms and face lifted up to the God he enthusiastically worshiped. The transformation was unbelievable. We were thrilled.

Several weeks later, a group of strangers stood at our church doors, waiting to come in. I hurried over to welcome them and asked how they had heard about our little church that met in a public school's cafeteria. They explained they were siblings of Chip. "Something big has happened to him," they told me. "We had to come and find out what in the world was going on."

God had done a wonderful thing in their brother's life. Joy, love, and peace had flooded his soul. You just couldn't miss it. And it drew his extended family in like moths to a flame.

I couldn't help but think of Chip as I mused over Peter's central idea. As Christians, we have the power to compel or repel people who are looking for God. We're here to represent him to a world living in darkness and despair. Our genuine and humble interactions with people seeking Christ as well as with other believers can make a difference in their receptiveness to the truth of the gospel.

Why Was Submission So Important to Winning Unbelieving Neighbors for Christ?

In Greco-Roman times, the family unit was considered foundational to a healthy society. Aristotle had outlined three pairs of relationships within a typical household: husband and wife, father and children, and master and slave.[2] This "household code" was found frequently in other contemporary secular writings. Lucy Peppiatt writes: "It is not possible to fathom the full import of the household codes, therefore, unless we understand that they had sociopolitical meaning and were not simply for private, individual homes."[3]

Roman aristocracy felt any deviation from the accepted norm was a threat to their power base. Therefore, a religion suspected of negatively influencing the status quo was closely monitored, especially when it urged the upward mobility of what were inferior elements in society, like former slaves, foreigners, and women.[4] One ancient writer stated: "Preserve the present order, and do not desire any change, knowing that revolutions inevitably destroy states and lay waste the homes of the people."[5] The Senate passed laws to keep social boundaries in place. High on the list was protecting against the social advancement of freedmen.[6]

With expected behavior firmly ensconced in society, both Paul and Peter addressed their instructions to families within that same format. A household code (with a Christian twist) is found in Colossians, Ephesians, and here in 1 Peter. Remember, Peter's central point was

---

2. Craig Keener, *Paul, Women, and Wives* (Grand Rapids: Baker, 1992), 146.
3. Lucy Peppiatt, *Rediscovering Scripture's Vision for Women* (Downers Grove, IL: InterVarsity Press, 2019), 98.
4. Keener, *Paul, Women, and Wives*, 139.
5. Keener, *Paul, Women, and Wives*, 144.
6. Keener, *Paul, Women, and Wives*, 144.

that his readers should be purposeful in how they lived out their household code, in hopes that their actions would speak louder than words and keep their unbelieving society from misunderstanding the nature of Christianity.

Peter gives several practical applications to his timeless principle.[7] The first of these is in submitting to secular government authority, officials sent by the king to keep order in their communities. Peter's readers are to be known as people who "honor all people, love the brotherhood, fear God, honor the king" (1 Peter 2:17). By doing this they will silence the ignorance of foolish men, who could mistake Christianity as a political movement threatening their society.

The second human-ordained institution Peter mentions is the relationship between slaves and masters. Slaves are to "be submissive to your masters with all respect, not only to those who are good and gentle, but also to those who are unreasonable. . . . But if when you do what is right and suffer for it you patiently endure it, this finds favor with God" (vv. 18–20 NASB1995). An attitude of submission was important even when the other person did not submit to God. A slave's obedience in such an unjust situation would speak volumes about the One to whom he was ultimately submitting: the Lord.

Peter then reminds his readers that this is exactly how Jesus responded to unjust human institutions. "While being reviled, He did not revile in return; while suffering, He uttered no threats, but kept entrusting Himself to Him who judges righteously" (v. 23 NASB1995). If they were following the example of Jesus Christ, even in unfair circumstances, they would do the same.

---

7. This structure is made clear through Peter's use of chiasm in 1 Peter 2:13–3:7:
    A "Submit yourselves for the Lord's sake to every human institution"
        B "Servants, be subject to your masters with all respect"
            C "Because Christ also suffered for you, leaving you an example,
                so that you would follow in His steps"
        B₁ "You wives, be subject to your own husbands"
    A₁ "You husbands . . . show [your wives] honor as a fellow heir of the grace of life"
    Part C puts Christ at the center and most important place in this chiasm. What surrounds his example are human applications of that point.

Now Peter moves to a third relationship: that of wives and husbands. He writes, "In the same way, you wives, be subject to your own husbands." Note the reason they are to do so: "so that even if any of them are disobedient to the word, they may be won over without a word by the behavior of their wives, as they observe your pure and respectful behavior" (3:1–2). He is speaking to the wives of men who have not yet believed in Christ. These wives are to do the same as slaves, who submit to their hard-hearted masters. When the wife submitted, it was not because he deserved it. She was ultimately submitting to her God. Any other behavior toward a nonbelieving husband would only confirm his suspicion that Christianity was seeking to destroy the foundation of Roman society by disrupting the family unit.

In Colossians, Paul makes it clear that submission is actually to their God, not people. Paul bookends the submission of wives, husbands, children, and slaves with two statements found in Colossians 3:17 and 3:23: "Whatever you do in word or deed, do everything in the name of the Lord Jesus, giving thanks through Him to God the Father. . . . Whatever you do, do your work heartily, as for the Lord and not for people."

Let's be clear: the wife is never told the husband has a rightful role of authority over her in 1 Peter 3. She is not submitting to him because he is more suitable to lead. (In fact, he is not even a believer!) She should choose to align herself with God's desire for her husband: that he would come to a saving faith and trust in Christ alone. Submitting to her husband will model that kind of trust in God for him.

What Does Peter Mean by Submit?

Let's review what we discovered about submission (*hypotasso*) in Ephesians 5. Remember, submission is not obedience. The *Theological Dictionary of the New Testament* defines *submission* as "readiness to renounce one's own will for the sake of others, . . . and to give precedence to others."[8] We saw Paul urging the Philippian church to

---

8. Kittel and Friedrich, *TDNT*, 41.

mutually submit with this plea: "Make my joy complete by being of the same mind, maintaining the same love, united in spirit, intent on one purpose. Do nothing from selfishness or empty conceit, but with humility consider one another as more important than yourselves; do not merely look out for your own personal interests, but also for the interests of others" (Phil. 2:2–4).

Peter has the same thing in mind as Paul, which is putting aside our desire for ourselves in the interest of serving another. But here is Peter's additional thrust: that attitude of submission is important even to people who are not mutually submitting to you. That includes Roman government authorities, hard-hearted masters, and unbelieving husbands. While those circumstances might be harder, it was still appropriate kingdom behavior.

We can confirm this by looking at what else Peter has to say about women in the rest of his letter.

What Was Peter's General Attitude toward Women?

Peter spent a lot of time in his epistle speaking to men and women as a unified group. By doing this, he equalized the sexes in what they had through Christ.

- Both were redeemed with precious blood (1 Peter 1:18–19). In real estate, a home is valued by how much someone is willing to pay for it. God paid for our redemption with his most precious thing: his only begotten Son. Both men's and women's value has been determined by the extravagant price he paid.
- Peter expected both men and women to "long for the pure milk of the word, so that by it you may grow in respect to salvation" (2:2). Knowledge was not just for the men, but equally encouraged among the women.
- All believers are "living stones . . . being built up as a spiritual house" (2:5). Every believer is an important and significant part of the kingdom God is erecting. In a wall, each stone has

its unique place, a part of the greater thing Christ calls his church.

- Men and women are a part of the "holy priesthood," a people for God's own possession to offer up "spiritual sacrifices" (2:5). We have an equal calling as priests, purposed to bring others into a relationship with God.

- Finally, Peter tells husbands that their wives are fellow heirs (3:7). Men and women share equally with Christ in his inheritance. No one is valued above the other.

How Does the Example of Sarah Add to Peter's Call to Submit?

Peter tells the wives, "Sarah obeyed Abraham, calling him lord; and you have proved to be her children if you do what is right without being frightened by any fear" (1 Peter 3:6). He picks an interesting example, since in the story of Abraham and Sarah, Abraham actually complied with Sarah's instructions more than once. The second time, God even told Abraham to listen to his wife and do what she says (see Gen. 16:2; 21:12).

The only time Sarah is recorded in Scripture calling Abraham "my lord" is in Genesis 18:12. It happened when she overheard a visitor[9] tell her husband, "I will certainly return to you at this time next year; and behold, your wife Sarah will have a son."

Sarah was long past the age of childbearing. When she heard the stranger's promise, she laughed to herself. She thought, "After I have become old, am I to have pleasure, *my lord* being old also?" (Gen. 18:10, 12, emphasis mine).

She was stunned when the stranger seemed to hear her internal response. He said, "Why did Sarah laugh, saying, 'Shall I actually give birth to a child, when I am so old?' Is anything too difficult for the Lord? At the appointed time I will return to you, at this time next year, and Sarah will have a son" (18:13–14).

---

9. A stranger who was either an angel or the preincarnate Christ.

Struck with sudden fear at hearing her thoughts supernaturally voiced out loud, Sarah stepped into the doorway and attempted to deny her laughter. But it was a futile effort. The stranger firmly responded: "You did laugh" (v. 15).

Sometime after the strangers took their leave, Abraham pulled up tent stakes and moved his family compound south to the outskirts of the Negev Desert and settled there. He spread the word that Sarah was his sister (presumably out of fear that someone would kill him to own her).[10] By doing this, he left Sarah vulnerable, and the king in that place, Abimelech, did indeed take Sarah for his own. The Lord intervened and Sarah was returned to Abraham.

While captive, did Sarah inform Abimelech of her marital status? It doesn't appear so, since Abimelech responds to God's revelation of this fact with "Did he not himself say to me, 'She is my sister'? And she herself said, 'He is my brother.'" (Gen. 20:5). So apparently Sarah stayed silent about Abraham's lie even in the face of impending disgrace. She submitted to her "lord."

Hebrews records her submission and clarifies where she ultimately put her trust: "By faith even Sarah herself received ability to conceive, even beyond the proper time of life, *since she considered Him faithful who had promised*" (Heb. 11:11, emphasis mine). Sarah's submission was not to her fallible husband. Though Sarah, too, was fallible, her submission was to the God she chose to trust. Peter is asking wives to follow her example in trusting God's purposes.

This gives us Peter's definition of a gentle and quiet spirit, by the way. The word translated *gentle*, is the same word that Jesus used in his Sermon on the Mount: "Blessed are the *meek*, for they will inherit the earth" (Matt. 5:5 NIV, emphasis mine). Meekness is not weakness. It is voluntarily placing one's power under someone else's control.[11]

---

10. This had happened before: in Genesis 12, Abraham went to Egypt to escape famine and told her, "See now, I know that you are a beautiful woman; and when the Egyptians see you, they will say, 'This is his wife'; and they will kill me, but they will let you live" (Gen. 12:11–12).

11. *Thayer's Lexicon* explains, "Meekness toward God is that disposition of spirit in which we accept His dealings with us as good, and therefore without disputing

In this case, it is a wife giving over her power not to her husband but to God, trusting he will do the right thing by her. *Quiet* can also be translated *tranquil*.[12] At peace. Together, *meek* and *tranquil* make an attitude of peaceful submission to God, because one trusts him completely.

What Does Peter Tell the Husbands?

He begins his instruction to the husbands, "You husbands in the same way . . ." (1 Peter 3:7). What Peter is about to ask the husbands is within the same line of thought. Godly submission is expressed by giving honor to their wives. They should treat their wives with understanding: give her the same grace they would give themselves. She may not be as physically strong or big as him, but she is his equal; a fellow heir, in fact.[13]

Take note that "Peter does not instruct husbands to exercise any authority at all. In Peter's thinking, the relevant authority is God."[14] Just like the wives, husbands are ultimately serving God through their actions, whom Peter references with his warning: "So that your prayers will not be hindered" (1 Peter 3:7).

Finally, Peter summarizes his examples on submission with a statement for all believers: "To sum up, all of you be harmonious, sympathetic, loving, compassionate, and humble" (v. 8 NASB1995). These

---

or resisting. In the OT, the meek are those wholly relying on God rather than their own strength to defend against injustice. Thus, meekness toward evil people means knowing God is permitting the injuries they inflict, that He is using them to purify His elect, and that He will deliver His elect in His time (Isa. 41:17, Luke 18:1–8). Gentleness or meekness is the opposite to self-assertiveness and self-interest. It stems from trust in God's goodness and control over the situation. The gentle person is not occupied with self at all. This is a work of the Holy Spirit, not of the human will (Gal 5:23)." Joseph Thayer, "meek," *Thayer's Greek-English Lexicon of the New Testament* (Miami, FL: Stanford Publishing, 2017).

12. Interestingly, Paul also uses this word in 1 Tim. 2:2, where he urges both men and women to lead a "tranquil and quiet life."

13. Later Peter cautions all leaders to not "lord it over" others, but to lead by example (1 Peter 5:3). Why would husbands not be held to a similar standard?

14. Andrew Bartlett, *Men and Women in Christ: Fresh Light From the Biblical Texts* (London: Inter-Varsity Press, 2020), 104.

descriptions augment our understanding of what he has just been asking of his readers. The most effective way to demonstrate the heart of God for unbelievers is by interacting in love, God's kind of love, *agape* love, which does the right thing for someone with no expectation of a return. And when choosing to submit to each other, we align ourselves with God's purposes.[15]

One last note: in both cases of the slave and the wife, Peter in no way suggests God's approval of either human hierarchical institution. It is what it is in Roman society. Christians are to live for a higher power than Roman law. We submit to the will of God.

Good News for Today

Peter's timeless principle was about living in such a way that those who do not yet believe in Christ will observe us and understand we live for a higher power. This is a truth that can transcend all times and cultures.

How this gets played out, how we *apply* this principle to our lives, can look very different from generation to generation. In the first century, Peter's suggested applications were in the context of living in the age of the Roman Empire. Seeing that Christianity was not aiming to overthrow the structure of their peaceful society would remove an impediment for the unbelieving to trust in Christ.

Peter's applications concerning this principle were specific to their society. A good application of that same principle would look very different today, when done within the culture and time period of the twenty-first century.

It is for that reason that most Christians no longer literally wash each other's feet.

In Jesus's day, foot washing was a necessity when a guest arrived at a home. In that hot, arid climate, sandals were the footwear of

---

15. In Rom. 12:18, Paul voiced the same principle: "If possible, so far as it depends on you, be at peace with all people." Paul was very conscious of what his readers might inadvertently portray with their actions that could turn people away from the only source of their salvation.

choice. A guest arriving at a home would have come in with dusty, dry feet. Washing their feet would make guests much more comfortable during their stay. (Do you remember what a faux pas it was for Simon the Pharisee to *not* provide that comfort for Jesus and his disciples in his home? See Luke 7:36–50.)

Washing someone's feet was considered a demeaning task, most often assigned to the lowest of servants. This is why Peter strongly objected when Jesus prepared to do this for him. "Never shall You wash my feet!" he exclaimed.

Jesus's act was that of a self-proclaimed servant. Jesus explained, "If I do not wash you, you have no place with Me" (John 13:8). Jesus had earlier given them the principle behind his act of servanthood: "The one who is greatest among you must become like the youngest, and the leader like the servant" (Luke 22:26). Now he additionally explained, "So if I, the Lord and the Teacher, washed your feet, you also ought to wash one another's feet. . . . Truly, truly, I say to you, a slave is not greater than his master, nor is one who is sent greater than the one who sent him" (John 13:14, 16).

If we were to enact that same principle of servanthood today, I daresay the expression would look far different from Jesus's first-century application. Today, if I asked a guest in my home to take off their shoes and socks so I could wash their feet, it would likely feel to them like a violation of privacy or intrusion of personal space. To follow Jesus's example in servanthood today might look more like bringing someone a meal, giving a monetary gift anonymously, honoring someone with hospitality by looking to their needs, or quietly jumping in to sweep the floors or wash the dishes after a church function.

If what we do to enact a principle in Scripture is quirky or "off" according to our current society, we could be erecting a barrier to possible converts coming to Christ. Peter H. Davis, in his article "A Silent Witness in Marriage," writes:

> Interpretations that focus on the unilateral obedience or submission of wives to husbands, regardless of cultural context,

achieve the opposite of Peter's intention. Rather than promoting harmony with culture, they set Christian marriage partners at odds with culture and thus heighten the tension, and Christianity is perceived as undermining culture in a retrogressive way. This is precisely what 1 Peter is seeking to minimize.[16]

The principle of keeping our behavior excellent so as to win converts to Christ is universal. But the specific application of that universal truth will look different depending on the time and place it is carried out. We live in a society that values personal growth and the free exercise of strengths and abilities. Insisting that women operate primarily at home, always take subordinate roles at church, and not exercise their teaching or leadership gifts based on debatable interpretations can end up discouraging people of this generation from investigating the claims of Christ. We must never compromise on the clear teaching of the Bible. However, we must also live conscious of people observing us and trust God to take our humble efforts and use them for his glory.

In the 1950s and '60s, one of the best-known players in NFL football was Rosey Grier. He had an outstanding career as a defensive tackle, first with the New York Giants and then with the Los Angeles Rams. A man with a heart of gold, Rosey was keenly aware of being in the public eye.

Rosey once spoke to a group of NFL recruits about their influence as sports heroes. One recruit spoke out in protest. "I don't want to be a role model," he said.

Rosey replied, "Son, when you accepted the NFL draft, you stepped into that position. The only thing you have to decide now is what kind of role model you're going to be."

---

16. Peter H. Davids, "A Silent Witness in Marriage: 1 Peter 3:1–7," in *Discovering Biblical Equality*, ed. Ronald W. Pierce, Rebecca Merrill Groothuis, and Gordon D. Fee (Downers Grove, IL: IVP Academic, 2005), 236.

That reality has a particular ring of truth for believers in Christ. God has decided to reveal himself in this present age through his church. We are called to live lives that reflect who we are in Christ to the world around us. Paul urged the Philippians to live as "children of God above reproach in the midst of a crooked and perverse generation, among whom you appear as lights in the world, holding firmly the word of life" (Phil. 2:15–16).

Like it or not, we are on display for all to see. We must find ways to express our attitude of submission to God that will not be offensive in the twenty-first century and avoid keeping those who do not yet believe from seeking Jesus. What is a godly woman, according to 1 Peter 3? Someone who puts her needs aside in the interest of the needs of another. She lives in submission to God alone, following the example Jesus gave us, submitting even in the face of unfairness or an unbelieving husband. We must align ourselves with God's desire to see all people saved (see 2 Peter 3:9). In the end, it's all about the kingdom of God.

Conclusion

A few years ago, I recommended that a friend listen to a sermon of mine that was related to the topic we had just been discussing. I could see by the look on her face that she was conflicted. Having had the same training as I did in our youth, she found it inconceivable that I could ever think it appropriate for a woman to preach from the pulpit. She asked with genuine concern: did I just ignore those verses about women not teaching and being silent in the church?

I assured her that she knew me better than that. Of course I loved and respected the Word of God! Of course I knew it was Holy Spirit–inspired and absolutely true! Our different convictions on women preachers were not due to a lack of reverence for God's Word. What we were dealing with was a variance in interpretation.

I hope by reading this book you have seen ways to study a passage that can unlock its intended meaning. Looking up the original words, noticing what is emphasized by the author, studying the structure, carefully considering its immediate context, the context of where it occurs in its book, and how it contributes to the whole of the Old and New Testaments will all help us understand what a passage meant at the time it was written. We can then pull the timeless principle out of its ancient context and more accurately apply God's truth to our lives today.

Unfortunately, many people stop short after a superficial reading and decide the interpretation and application without a thorough study. Then they cherry-pick other passages and group them together to construct a theology or doctrine, arriving at a collective meaning none of them individually were meant to have.

There's no doubt that people are doing the best they can to understand God's Word and apply it correctly. The real problem lies in the interpretation principles they choose to employ. If not carefully studied, what they get from the text is far off the mark. And the applications of that error go even wider.

When NASA first sent men to the moon in 1969, the orbits of the earth and moon had to be taken into consideration. Calculations were made over and over again to be sure the trajectory of the spacecraft was exactly right. Because if they were even a degree off in their calculations, the spaceship would miss the moon by a wide margin.

Similarly, when you start with an incorrect scriptural understanding, by the time you reach an application, you may have entirely missed what God is asking you to do.

We've seen that happen all too often when it comes to interpreting pertinent passages on women. Scripture is approached with preconceived ideas that can make us see things that aren't even there in the text. Rather than the Spirit leading us into truth, we are subconsciously looking to validate traditions from another culture or our own ideas.

When men are assumed to be in power, and women are assumed to be followers, bad things happen. Wives are abused, both physically and emotionally. Women are restricted in their use of the spiritual gifts given to them by the Holy Spirit. Women in successful ministry are lambasted for speaking in front of men. People in high positions are given a pass for their ungodly behavior, even when in direct conflict with the Bible. Taking a bad doctrine to its inevitable conclusion misses the mark by a mile.

We have all seen power corrupt. Unfortunately, this is just as true in the church as it is in the world. Knowing our human propensity to grab for importance or self-glory, God designed the church to be different. Each member is to be significant and necessary to the group. Each is endowed with an ability meant to build up the body. We are designed to be an intermutual community, all of us completely dependent on God.

When we function as we were designed to function, the local body is healthy and thrives. People are encouraged to use their gifts to benefit their brothers and sisters. No one person is in power or domineering. Each looks to the needs of others. We are not self-centered, but Christ-centered.

The same is true for biblical marriages. Each spouse is primarily concerned with the needs of the other. They put themselves aside and do what they can to move the other forward into maturity in Christ. It is a partnership, not a hierarchy.

As I worked through these passages, a single idea continually struck me. The kingdom of God has never been about a hierarchy or power. It is not about those who are important and those who are not. Even the apostles did not think in those terms. The kingdom is about servanthood and humility. It is about considering others' needs over our own. No one is above the rest.

We were created equal, called to mutually submit for the sake of Christ. A grab for power (or a fight to keep power) goes against what Jesus taught. No one should think themselves above the rest. No one should think any kingdom citizen as "less than" or insignificant. Jesus exemplified this with every word and action: God's kingdom is different than the world.

We're called to something bigger. It is only when the church recognizes this that we can expect to be a light shining into the darkness. Keeping women back will only inhibit our impact on the world. True biblical men and women uphold kingdom values. They honor the Bible and what it teaches. When we align ourselves with God's agenda, he will use us for his glory. May we move in that direction, unencumbered by inaccurate interpretation and, even worse, self-serving agendas. Let's all rejoice and live in the freedom the truth brings. To God be the glory.

Acknowledgments

The Lord has been so faithful to put people in my path to move me along in my quest for a biblical perspective on women. There is a community on Facebook called "Biblical Christian Egalitarians" who have been a wonderful resource as I have worked through these passages. When I needed a story to flesh out my material, over seventy of them sent stories of personal experience that gave purpose and insight to my teaching. To all of you, I am grateful for your respect for God's Word and for the work you have personally done to come to a biblical understanding. I'm humbled by your friendship and encouragement.

I also thank those in my Masterminds Group and others in the Advanced Writers and Speakers Association. Iron sharpens iron, and our community builds up its members. Thank you for reading and reviewing my material as it developed. Your interest and enthusiasm are invaluable to me.

Two impressive leaders in support of women have been so generous with their time. Mimi Haddad and Monica Schmelter wrote endorsements that probably sold my book proposal. Mimi is the tireless, dedicated president of Christians for Biblical Equality, an international organization that is working toward equality for women all over the globe. It was while hearing her speak at a local event that I realized the key to this book was to write in love. Monica is a Christian television host (of "Bridges" on TCN) and a TV station manager. She has been enthusiastic about this book from the very beginning, and has so generously used her professional knowledge to help me in countless ways. For both of you, I humbly give thanks.

There are many who have shared their expertise with me. Davey Ermold, pastor and Greek and Hebrew expert, has assisted me through some tricky translation issues. Ron Pierce, in his online gender class with Biola, helped me finally break through 1 Corinthians 11 (which was no small feat!). Marg Mowczko, scholar and blogger, sent many edits that added accuracy and validity to this book. Linda Coleman, PhD, linguistic professor at the University of Maryland, was very helpful in her editing as well.

Many authors added to my understanding with books of their own. Writers like Lucy Peppiatt, Philip Payne, Richard and Catherine Kroeger, Craig Keener, Cynthia Westfall, Michelle Lee-Barnewall, and Rebecca Groothuis are part of a great army of scholars and teachers who have blazed an ever-widening trail for those seeking a true biblical perspective. I am honored and humbled to stand shoulder to shoulder with all of you. Thank you for following God with your gifts. We are all grateful.

To the body of believers at New Hope Chapel, I again thank you for giving me opportunity to use my gifts in ways (as a woman) I never dreamed possible. Your unconditional love is everything to me and to Steve. We can't imagine life without you!

And finally, to my husband, Steve, words cannot express what an enormous encouragement and help you are to me. I have loved our many discussions over this material. Your support, from excellent editing to exchange of ideas to overall enthusiasm, kept me going in those dark COVID-19 days as I wrote. I could not love you more.

Bibliography

Adler, Mortimer J. *Great Books of the Western World, Volume 3.* Edinburgh: Encyclopedia Britannica Inc., 1952.

Aristotle, *Metaphysics,* quoted in *The Women's History of the World: How Radicals, Rebels, and Everywoman Revolutionized the Last 200 Years* by Rosalind Miles. Topsfield, MA: Salem House, 1989.

Arnold, Clinton E. *Ephesians, Exegetical Commentary on the New Testament.* Grand Rapids: Zondervan, 2010.

Bailey, Kenneth E. "Women in the New Testament: A Middle Eastern Cultural View." *Anglican Evangelical Journal for Theology and Mission,* Vol. 6, no. 1 (2000).

Barrett, C. K. *The First Epistle to the Corinthians.* Harper's New Testament Commentaries. New York: Harper & Row, 1968.

Bartlett, Andrew. *Men and Women in Christ: Fresh Light From the Biblical Texts.* London: Inter-Varsity Press, 2020.

Baur, Walter. *A Greek-English Lexicon of the New Testament and Other Early Christian Literature,* 3rd ed., ed. Frederick William Danker, W. F. Arndt, and F. W. Gingrich. Chicago: University of Chicago Press, 2000.

Bible History. "Temple Warning Inscription." 2020. https://www.bible-history.com/archaeology/israel/temple-warning.html.

Bilezikian, Gilbert. *Beyond Sex Roles.* Grand Rapids: Baker Academic, 2006.

Bridges, Vincent. "Paganism in Provence." *Journal of the Western Mystery Tradition* 1, no. 6 (2004).

Bristow, John Temple. *What Paul Really Said about Women*. San Francisco: HarperCollins, 1991.

Brown, Francis, S. R. Driver, and Charles Briggs, eds. *The Brown-Driver-Briggs Hebrew and English Lexicon* (BDB). Peabody, MA: Hendrickson, 2006.

Bruce, F. F. *1 and 2 Corinthians*. New Century Bible Commentary. London: Marshall, Morgan & Scott, 1971.

———. *The Epistles to the Colossians, to Philemon, and to the Ephesians*. The New International Commentary on the New Testament. Grand Rapids: Eerdmans, 1984.

Brueggemann, Walter. *Genesis, Interpretation: A Bible Commentary for Teaching and Preaching*. Louisville, Kentucky: John Knox Press, 1982.

Carter, Jimmy. *A Call to Action: Women, Religion, Violence, and Power*. New York: Simon & Schuster, 2014.

Cohick, Lynn H. *Women in the World of the Earliest Christians*. Grand Rapids: Baker Academic, 2009.

———. "A Silent Witness in Marriage: 1 Peter 3:1–7." *Discovering Biblical Equality*. Edited by Ronald W. Pierce, Rebecca Merrill Groothuis, and Gordon D. Fee. Downers Grove, IL: IVP Academic, 2005.

Davids, Peter H. *The First Epistle of Peter*. The New International Commentary on the New Testament. Grand Rapids: Eerdmans, 1990.

Edwards, Bob and Helga. *The Equality Workbook: Freedom in Christ from the Oppression of Patriarchy*. Self-published, CreateSpace, 2016.

Epstein, Randi Hutter. *Get Me Out: A History of Childbirth from the Garden of Eden to the Sperm Bank*. New York: W. W. Norton & Company, Inc., 2010.

Fee, Gordon. *The First Epistle to the Corinthians*. The New International Commentary on the New Testament. Grand Rapids: Eerdmans, 1987.

Fleming, Bruce C. E. *Women and Men in the Light of Eden.* Self-published, Xulon Press, 2011.

Garland, David E. *1 Corinthians.* Baker Exegetical Commentary on the New Testament. Grand Rapids: Baker Academic, 2003.

Grudem, Wayne A. *1 Peter.* Tyndale New Testament Commentaries. Downers Grove, IL: IVP Academic, 1988.

Hess, Richard S. "Equality With and Without Innocence." *Discovering Biblical Equality: Complementarity Without Hierarchy.* Edited by Ronald W. Pierce, Rebecca Merrill Groothuis, and Gordon D. Fee. Downers Grove, IL: IVP Academic, 2005.

Horton, Haley. "The Unavoidable Link Between Patriarchal Theology and Spiritual Abuse." *CBE International* (blog). January 13, 2021. Accessed November 23, 2021. https://www.cbe international.org/resource/article/mutuality-blog-magazine /unavoidable-link-between-patriarchal-theology-and.

Hurley, James B. *Man and Woman in Biblical Perspective.* Grand Rapids: Zondervan, 1981.

Isocrates. *Loeb Classical Library: Works.* Translated by George Norlin and Larue van Hook. 3 vols. London: Wm. Heinemann; New York: Putnam's Sons, 1925–61.

Josephus. *Josephus: The Complete Works.* Translated by William Whiston. Nashville: Thomas Nelson, 1998.

"Judaism in Ephesus." *Ephesus.* https://www.ephesus.us/ephesus/juda ism_in_ephesus.htm.

Keener, Craig S. *And Marries Another: Divorce and Remarriage in the Teaching of the New Testament.* Grand Rapids: Baker Academic, 1991.

———. *The IVP Bible Background Commentary.* Downers Grove, IL: InterVarsity Press, 1993.

———. "Learning in the Assemblies: 1 Corinthians 14:34–35." *Discovering Biblical Equality: Complementarity Without Hierarchy.* Edited by Ronald W. Pierce, Rebecca Merrill Groothuis, and Gordon D. Fee. Downers Grove, IL: IVP Academic, 2005.

———. *Paul, Women, and Wives: Marriage and Women's Ministry in the Letters of Paul*. Grand Rapids: Baker Academic, 1992.

Kent, Homer A., Jr. *The Pastoral Epistles: Studies in 1, 2 Timothy and Titus*. Winona Lake, IN: BMH Books, 1982.

Kittel, Gerhard and Gerhard Friedrich, eds. *Theological Dictionary of the New Testament*. 10 vols. Grand Rapids: Eerdmans, 1972.

Kraeger, Shane M. "Toward a Mediating Understanding of Tongues: A Historical and Exegetical Examination of Early Literature." *Eleutheria* 1, no. 1 (2010).

Kroeger, Richard Clark and Catherine Clark Kroeger. *I Suffer Not a Woman to Teach*. Grand Rapids: Baker, 1992.

Layton, Bentley, trans. "The Hypostasis of the Archons." *Early Christian Writings*, accessed November 17, 2020. http://www.earlychristianwritings.com/text/archons.html.

Lee-Barnewall, Michelle. *Neither Complementarian nor Egalitarian: A Kingdom Corrective to the Evangelical Gender Debate*. Grand Rapids: Baker Academic, 2016.

Lotz, Anne Graham. "Jesus Calls Women to Serve and Lead." *Washington Post*, September 21, 2008. http://newsweek.washingtonpost.com/onfaith/guestvoices/2008/09/jesus_calls_women_to_serve_and.html.

Marshall, I. Howard. "Mutual Love and Submission in Marriage." *Discovering Biblical Equality: Complementarity Without Hierarchy*. Edited by Ronald W. Pierce, Rebecca Merrill Groothuis, and Gordon D. Fee. Downers Grove, IL: IVP Academic, 2005.

Mathews, Alice. *Gender Roles and the People of God: Rethinking What We Were Taught about Men and Women in the Church*. Grand Rapids: Zondervan, 2017.

Morris, Leon. *1 Corinthians*. Tyndale New Testament Commentaries. Grand Rapids: Eerdmans, 1985.

Mowczko, Marg. "The Twelve Apostles Were All Male." *Marg Mowczko* (blog). May 2, 2012. Accessed November 12, 2021. https://margmowczko.com/the-twelve-apostles-were-all-male/.

Nyland, Ann Maxwell-Nithsdale. *The Source New Testament: With Extensive Notes on Greek Word Meaning.* Australia: Smith and Stirling Publishing, 2007.

Payne, Philip B. *Man and Woman, One in Christ: An Exegetical and Theological Study of Paul's Letters.* Grand Rapids: Zondervan, 2009.

Peppiatt, Lucy. *Rediscovering Scripture's Vision for Women: Fresh Perspectives on Disputed Texts.* Downers Grove, IL: InterVarsity Press, 2019.

———. *Unveiling Paul's Women: Making Sense of 1 Corinthians 11:2–16.* Eugene, OR: Cascade Books, 2018.

Philo. "De Opificio Mundi," in *Theological Dictionary of the New Testament.* Vol. 1. Edited by G. Kittel. Grand Rapids: Eerdmans, 1965.

Pierce, Ronald W. "Deborah: Troublesome Woman or Woman of Valor?" *Priscilla Papers* 32, no. 2 (Spring 2018).

———. "Women and Men in Christian Assembly: Theology of Gender." Lecture at Biola University, La Mirada, CA, April 2013. https://www.youtube.com/watch?v=lRW8dCfvaMg&list=PLYtrZmQ7NN0CRA-gWcqZOvB5nmUuJ6FNe&index=10.

Pierce, Ronald W., Rebecca Groothuis, and Gordon D. Fee, eds. *Discovering Biblical Equality: Complementarity Without Hierarchy.* Downers Grove, IL: IVP Academic, 2005.

Ritter, Tim. "Without Gender Equality, Our Gospel Has A Hole In It." *CBE International* (blog). October 9, 2018. Accessed November 12, 2021. https://www.cbeinternational.org/resource/article/mutuality-blog-magazine/without-gender-equality-our-gospel-has-hole-it.

Sheill, William. *Reading Acts: The Lector and the Early Christian Audience.* Leiden, Netherlands: Brill, 2004.

Thayer, Joseph, ed. *A Greek Lexicon of the New Testament.* New York: American Book Co., 1886.

———. *Thayer's Greek-English Lexicon of the New Testament.* Miami, FL: Stanford Publishing, 2017.

Waltke, Bruce J. *Genesis: A Commentary.* Grand Rapids: Zondervan, 2001.

Watson, Richard. "Nicolaitans." In Watson's Biblical & Theological Dictionary. Accessed November 12, 2021. https://www.studylight.org/dictionaries/wtd/n/nicolaitans.html.

Westfall, Cynthia Long. *Paul and Gender: Reclaiming the Apostle's Vision for Men and Women in Christ.* Grand Rapids: Baker Academic, 2016.

Winters, Robert W. *Accidental Medical Discoveries: How Tenacity and Pure Dumb Luck Changed the World.* New York: Skyhorse Publishing, 2016.

Youngblood, Ronald F., ed. *Nelson's New Illustration Bible Dictionary,* Nashville: Thomas Nelson, 1995.